PRACTICAL SPIRITUALITY

by John Randolph Price

A Quartus Book

Library of Congress Catalog Card Number 85-62275
International Standard Book Number 0-942082-06-0

Published by QUARTUS BOOKS
The Quartus Foundation for Spiritual Research, Inc.
P.O. Box 26683
Austin, Texas 78755

Printed in the United States of America

This book is lovingly dedicated to the members of the Planetary Commission throughout the world.

ACKNOWLEDGEMENT

The Acknowledgement Page in books is reserved for the expression of recognition and gratitude for assistance in the preparation of the book. Accordingly, I wish to express my appreciation to the delightful angel of my life—my wife, Jan—for sharing her fantastic Love, Light, Wisdom and Energy...to my mother, Eva, the beautiful soul who taught me the meaning of the word *practical* when I was a boy...to my daughters, Susan and Leslie, whose support and encouragement mean so much...and to Maggi, my 4-legged best friend who lights up my life by showing me how to play.

CONTENTS

INTRODUCTION

Someone once asked me to describe the common denominators of the Awakened Ones (Superbeings) we had met, and I promptly listed five characteristics. Later I discussed these attributes in our workshops with this commentary:

First of all, their priority system is different from most other people. Whether we realize it or not, most people are content to just "get by" — to accept sickness or ill health, or lack and limitation, or strained and broken relationships, or futility and unfulfillment. They tend to accept these experiences as their lot in life. And even when they get involved in metaphysics and become a part of the New Thought movement, they still keep their cop-outs. They blame their lack of mastery on karma, the will of God, the race consciousness, their own past mistakes, the idea that they are being tested, or on their lack of understanding.

Perhaps some of the Superbeings also went through the pity pot and blame syndrome, but they didn't stay there long. They made a definite commitment to mastery, and I can just see them standing up straight and strong and making their declarations with words like these: "I refuse to accept anything but perfect harmony in my life. I will not be sick...I will not be poor...and by God, and through God, and with God, I will shatter these illusions and build a new model of reality—a new world of peace, joy, abundance, radiant health, loving relationships, true place success and fulfillment!"

And so they established the priority of achieving mastery over this world, and they never lost sight of the goal. They soon realized that through the grace of God they could rise above all karmic influences...that the will of God is a kingdom on earth as it is in heaven...that from the Light of their own indwelling Christ they could be shielded from the negative influences of the race consciousness...that every mistake could be cancelled out through the acceptance of God's forgiveness...that God knows everyone so there is no need to test anyone...and that it is not the individual's understanding but God's Understanding that comes forth as the miracle-working Power.

Having a *spiritual priority in life* is the first apparent difference you'll find with these "miracle-workers." And the second common denominator is a radiant sense of *unconditional love* manifesting outwardly as pure joy—and they are so filled with the love and joy of living that they actually repel anything of a negative nature that might come their way.

The third characteristic is *peace*. Knowing that stress and tension will close the door to their good, they practice the art of peaceful relaxation from morning until night. And while they may work hard, they do it with a sense of ease. They draw forth that deep peace from within and they live and move and have their being in a center of serenity, regardless of what is going on around them.

The fourth is *right judgement*. While still operating in the world of the third dimension, they used common sense, and as they moved into spiritual consciousness that common sense was transformed into spiritual wisdom. And if they wobbled back and forth between the two planes, which happens until there is a "locking in" to the Christ Presence within, they used discernment and followed every prompting of their intuition.

And the fifth common denominator is *the practice of the Presence of God*. They know that God is individualized as each one, and so they practice the art of Self-Awareness. They understand that cosmic law always operates on the basis of an individual's NOW identity, so they take on the identity of the Master Self within and work with the law as co-creators.

After I had discussed these characteristics with people for about a year, I suddenly realized that I had left out a very important attribute: The Awakened Ones, the Evolved Souls, the Superbeings are all *very practical people!* While we may think of them as "mystical masters of the Fourth Dimension" (as one Quartus member put it), we must also consider them as Spiritual Pragmatists. They have moved from theoretical spirituality to practical spirituality, because they are applying the Truth they know to transform illusion into Reality. They are the *doers* of the Aquarian Age, architects of the future and builders of the new civilization. And the doing, the designing and the building are being accomplished by the right use of affirmative prayer, spiritual treatments and meditation...by living the spiritual life moment by moment...by being in accord and cooperating with Spirit...by putting total trust in God and living life fearlessly...by uniting mind and heart and going forth with great enthusiasm to accomplish that which must be done in the world at this time, always listening to the inner Guidance...and by moving through the 12 Doors of initiation and stepping out and up as a Master.

The chapters in this book covering these subjects are a compilation from the Quartus Report articles that I have written in the past year—each one being expanded with additional thoughts, ideas and understanding. Let's use this material in a program of *practical spirituality* and move from third dimensional "getting by" to Fourth Dimensional Living. As we do, more Light will be released into the mass consciousness and Planet Earth will begin to respond to that higher and purer vibration.

Later in the book I say that "our brothers and sisters from the civilizations of the stars, the Masters of Wisdom, the guardian angels, and the devas of all the kingdoms are all joyfully anticipating the penetrative thrust, the breakthrough, of Light into the race consciousness." Since that mass illumination will be made up of individual lights, isn't it time now for us all to get turned on?

Let's do it...and then let's meet on the mountain for the procession. See you there!

John Randolph Price

1

Prophecy, Principle and Pragmatism

In my imagination I found myself on a high cliff standing about twenty yards from the precipice—talking to an Awakened One who called himself Asher. And I said, "You have the gift of prophecy. What do you see for our world? What is your vision of the future?"

Asher replied, "Walk toward the edge of the cliff."

"May I ask why?"

"Just do as I say. Walk slowly now and listen carefully to my words. *If you continue on the same course, you will soon step off the precipice and plunge to the depths below.* That, my friend, is a prophecy."

I stopped a few feet from the edge and returned to my companion. "You changed directions. So much for prophecy. I can only tell you what will happen *if.*"

"Let's say that the world will continue on its present course. What then?"

The old master sat down on the ground and motioned for me to do the same. After several minutes of silence he addressed my question. "Individual man is a most unpredictable animal, yet collectively as a unified consciousness he is constantly declaring that which shall come to pass. Consider the snowflake. Each is a divine original, never announcing its intentions. But an avalanche is quite a different matter. The large mass composed of countless snow crystals moves down the mountainside, speeding toward its destination below—a small village perhaps. The outcome? Quite predictable, wouldn't you say?"

"If the snowslide could not be stopped in some way, the community could possibly be destroyed."

Asher nodded in agreement. "The mass consciousness must be stopped, or shall we say 'changed,' otherwise the cataclysm will occur and this planetary community will cease to exist—at least as we know it today."

"We can do it," I said. "I refuse to accept any idea that we can't clean up our mess. The race mind can be penetrated and its vibration changed through sufficient prayer and meditation. I know this with all my heart. Otherwise, the whole concept of the Planetary Commission is meaningless."

Asher stared at me intently, then said: "Here, take this rock and pitch it over there." I followed his instruction. "Now understand that there is a difference between prophecy and principle. The rock fell to the earth because of gravitational attraction, a natural law. There is certainty here, not possibilities or prevailing tendencies on which predictions are made. The rock *had* to fall. Where principles are involved, particularly those that are a part of the cosmic tapestry, the action is predetermined by law and is therefore exact. Not so with prophecies, whether from John the Elder, Nostradamus, or myself. They are but probabilities from 'readings' of logical outcomes of consciousness in motion. Now let us look at the future, the parts that are both pliant and fixed."

I interrupted. "I don't like to think of anything, particularly anything negative, as fixed and inevitable. Are not all things possible with God?"

"No. It is not possible for God to compromise truth or violate principle. To properly use that statement, you must bring it down to the personal level. You can say 'With God, all good things are possible in my life as Spirit works through my spiritual consciousness to harmonize my world.' But even then the natural laws are not suspended on the physical plane. Rather, the principle of divine order is fulfilled as you are seemingly 'lifted above' the level of the problem and it is no longer a part of your experience."

"So what you are saying is that no matter what the prediction may be, whether based on prophecy or law, there is a way out...that by becoming one with the Christ Consciousness we can move above the effect of so-called 'natural' causes, and that prophecies affecting humanity can be changed through an alteration of the collective consciousness."

Asher smiled. "Connect the numbers and you will have a picture. You make it sound so easy. A person could visualize a house built on the land, but he could not physically **live** in the house until it was completed. It is on this point that I take issue with so many people who profess to be 'New Agers.' Many can see the way and describe the path, but few are actually committed to the journey...to the actual building of a new home for mankind. How many are working to elevate consciousness in a compelling sense of *preparation* for coming events? And how many are doing this selflessly and without avarice—to purposely awaken the race mind?"

As I tried to answer, his raised hand signaled silence. He was deep in thought for several minutes. When he began to speak again his voice was very low.

"Listen closely," he said. "Many changes will soon take place in the world. I am not referring to a climax resulting from man's inhumanity to man, at least not specifically. While this cruelty will seem to accelerate for a time, the major changes will take place through the force of nature as she seeks, by law, to reclaim her planet. Is not order the first law of the universe? Order means balance, and nature is out of balance. She must regain her equilibrium. To do this she must eliminate the force of negative energy emanating from the race consciousness of man that is causing the imbalance — to relieve the pressure. In a way, you could say that nature will become a part of the Planetary Commission to heal the planet. Had more people risen to a higher level of consciousness before this time, the spiritual energy would have corrected the imbalance and nature would not have to take matters into her own hands."

"You make it sound a little ominous," I said. "And I think you're forgetting about the effect that the world healing meditation will have on conditions."

"I am not forgetting anything," Asher replied. "In your book announcing the Planetary Commission you say something about all the love and spiritual energy that will be released into the race mind—and that the spell for the majority of mankind 'will break up like the thawing of a frozen lake in springtime.' Thawing takes time, as you allude to later in the book when you write that 'the massive spiritual treatment of the race mind on Healing Day will not automatically pick us all up and drop us right in the middle of the Garden.' Are you not saying that this is the *beginning* phase of the building process, rather than the completion of the cycle?"

"Yes, but I like to think that the building process will be done in peace and harmony, and that the activities of the Commission will result in a dramatic change for the good of all mankind."

Asher seemed to be looking right through me. "I will tell you what I see. Through the spiritual work of millions of people...many being totally unaware of the Planetary Commission...there will be a uniting of spiritually minded people on the planet through a particular vibration in the ethers. This fusing of energies, which will reach a peak on December 31, 1986, will remove the threat of global war but will not eliminate all local hostilities. It will also cause dramatic advances in scientific discoveries, revamp the concept of established 'religion and church,' and serve as a ring of protection for more than three billion people. That number represents those already on the spiritual path, in addition to those in the ascendency toward a spiritual consciousness, as opposed to a continuing descent into the mire of materiality."

"Pardon me for interrupting again," I said, "but you've only covered slightly more than half of the world's population. What about the others?"

"Nature will soon enter her cleansing cycle. Those who reject the earth changes with an attitude of 'it can't happen here' will experience the greatest emotion of fear and panic, followed by rage and violent action. These individuals, with their lower vibratory rates, will be removed during the next two decades. Those who *expect* change and face it calmly with faith will move through it virtually untouched and will be the builders of the future."

"What I am hearing is both horrible and hopeful," I said. "I know that one of the most serious problems we have today is overpopulation, but wiping more than 2-billion people off the face of the earth is a little drastic, don't you think?"

Asher replied, "I can only tell you what I see at the present time. I might add . . . who are we to say that those people did not volunteer to be a part of the destruction and regeneration — for the purpose of soul growth? Never forget that each individual has free will and free choice."

Something Asher had said earlier was on my mind. "What did you mean when you said that 'nature' was going to play a role in the Planetary Commission?"

Asher: "Nature will act as a catalyst in the uniting of people, a bringing together of men and women with a common goal . . . to seek Light rather than darkness, to love rather than hate. Through adversity will come unity."

Asher obviously picked up the feeling of sadness in my heart. "My friend, do not despair. Do you recall the example of the falling rock? This was the law of gravitation at work. Without it, chaos would reign in the universe. So it is an unfailing principle. But does not a feather also fall to the earth following the same law of attraction? Do you see my point? If the rock is changed to a feather, the principle is not violated — only the mass is transformed. As the mass of negative energy, the force of change, is moving toward experience, its weight and velocity can be altered, transmuted, from intensely violent occurences to *manageable* conditions on the planet. How? Through a change in individual consciousness, and secondly, by applying that uplifted consciousness to world service. That is the most *practical* way to change the rock into a feather."

"Can you be more specific?"

Asher: "In case you do not know the definition of pragmatism, let me tell you. It means *a practical approach to problems.* Now what could be more practical for an individual than to raise his consciousness to where he is living above the level of any difficulty? And what could be more practical for the planet than for the individual to share that purer energy for the good of all? Theory is absorbing. Intellectualizing is fascinating. But now is the time for individual action—for *doing.* It is interesting that 'practical' and 'pragmatic' come from the Greek word *prattein,* meaning *to do."*

I said, "It sounds like you're talking about working *with* Spirit in the co-creation process?"

"Exactly! That is the activity of a spiritual pragmatist. He knows that Spirit finds entrance into the phenomenal world only through the consciousness of man. Therefore he corrects and trains consciousness to be a fit channel. Nothing is more practical than daily meditation, prayer and higher visioning. Nothing is more practical than eliminating fear and loving unconditionally. There is nothing more practical than living a spiritual life!"

Asher had picked up a rock and was holding it tightly in his hand. It was several minutes before he spoke again. Finally he said, "If fifty million people actually participate in the world healing meditation on December 31, 1986, nature will be greatly tranquilized and the necessity for massive cleansing will be alleviated. And the positives I mentioned will be enhanced. You see, the scenario I gave you was based on a much smaller number combining their energies for the good of the world, for that is what I now see. Millions more must be reached and influenced if the rock is to become a feather. Look to the Quartus members first and fan out from there. Journalists must write about the Commission for the mass media. Those in broadcasting and film production must spread the word. Every counselor, seminar leader, healer, minister, practitioner, author, publisher, educator, teacher, and writer must speak and write of the Commission. Every spiritual group must rise above competitive attitudes and join together in a spirit of cooperation for world healing. Egos must be shrink-wrapped. Each individual must contact those with ears to hear and eyes to see. There is no necessity of 'promoting' Quartus, the book relating to the commission, or the author. The Commission is not a 'merchandising' activity—it belongs to everyone. People talking to people need only encourage the joining together in prayer for the world at the appointed time. Why say more? And the words of the prayer are not as important as the releasing of the energies from a heart of love and a will dedicated to good-for-all."

I said, "The salvation of the world really does depend on each one of us, doesn't it?"

There was great light in Asher's eyes as he said, "Those who are looking for a savior can find one by looking in the mirror. Do your part in helping people grow by teaching *practical* spirituality, and they will realize that the redeemer and deliverer lives within each heart. And then, as each one releases the radiant energy to go forth on wings of Love, all things will be made new. That is the *practical* way of salvation...the most efficient, judicious, functional and realistic way...not only for the individual, but for the planet."

Then Asher threw the rock into the air. Strange. As it reached its zenith and began to fall, it seemed to float to earth...just like a feather! I turned within and tears of joy came forth, along with two simple words..."Thank you!"

I got up and walked outside into the bright sunshine. As I reached the boatdock, hundreds of fish began swimming in circles waiting for a few goodies that might be tossed their way. Lorien Bell, the member services director for Quartus, shares her lunch with these friends each day, and they have become her totally trusting pets. I know that if she ever caught me on the dock with a fishing pole, I'd receive a swift kick in the pants and her underwater friends would have a new swimming companion.

Standing there looking at the lake, the whole panorama of nature filled my mind and heart with its beauty and love-liness...the water, the fish, the squirrels playing in the trees, the flowers, the birds, the blue sky...and again that feeling of gratitude welled up inside. I love this world, and I don't like to think of destruction and devastation. Thank God we will have feathers instead of rocks.

As I was pondering these thoughts, something within said, "Do not fail to see that which has been predicted, yet know that it can be changed. Many voices are clamoring to be heard, and those with a message of finality and hopelessness seem to be the loudest. It has been written that 'where there is no hope, there can be no endeavor.' Messages must be acknowledged, then countered with encouragement. 'Yes' to the vision, 'no' to the manifestation. The picture of what has to be changed must be presented in order for it to be changed. Becoming an ostrich will not alter the picture. Show the picture as the object of positive endeavors, and provide optimistic expectations concerning the alterations."

That made sense to me because in so many instances we are shown the problem followed by a footnote indicating that "it's too late to do anything about it now." So what I think the inner voice was telling me was to show you the picture based on some of the information we have received, and then for us as a group to say: "Okay, we've seen the picture — and now that we know the possibilities, we can put the fear of the unknown to rest and get busy doing what has to be done. Instead of 'unity through adversity,' let's have it through love, joy and a commitment to service. Now let's go lift our consciousness and turn rocks into feathers!"

With that kind of attitude we can look without fear at the scenario that has been developed by extraterrestrials, non-physical beings, scientists, scholars, journalists, metaphysicians and mystics — speaking through trance mediums, newspaper reports, books and lectures. And no matter how ugly, evil or fearful the picture appears, we can look at it calmly and know that we have the power to change the script and project a new Reality on the screen of the outer world.

But we can't do it with our heads in the sand. In order to develop alternatives, we must see what has been "written" — and then work in the most *practical* way to reveal new solutions, new answers.

Regarding the channeled information, we have received many messages from Quartus members and others around the world, and each report has been numbered and filed according to the date the information came through. For example, an entity speaking through "Howard" on April 3, 1976 carries the file number of 4376. For the purpose of this review, we have compiled brief excerpts from Reports 4376 through 102084.

A look at the future for the purpose of making changes

Excerpts from Channeled Reports — representing the key thoughts.

It is urgent that you plan now for this decade for the one following will bring much suffering. You are moving into the darkness of oppression, a limiting of what you know as individual freedom. A police state? Yes, we see that...and many underground movements to support one another in Christ. Watch for signs after middle of 80's decade. Time is short. There is a great deal to be done. The earth is going into a new octave (which) will bring trial, tribulation and tests. Your nuclear devices are in danger of being ripped open by earthquakes, by volcanic activity. Many of the major faults that go up to the center of the U.S., the East Coast as well as the West Coast, there is a network like a spider web. You have no idea what lies under your earth crust, and as this action is created by volcanic eruption or by the major shifting of the plates under the ocean, or the major pulling apart of the rifts, sea water will be coming up. The continent is rising in your Atlantic Ocean. From Bimini, from Bermuda, all the way up...many areas will be under intense flooding and devastation...tidal waves of water that you could not conceive of. The storms will become super storms. Many tornados...incredible winds. The lakes that you have, called the Great Lakes, will empty into the Gulf. You can experience more fires—arson, yes...many fires from lightning. Your tropical forests are being destroyed, your air and water are polluted. Agriculture will suffer bringing on food shortages. All nations have karma. All nations must reap as they have sown. The catastrophies are scheduled and they will come about. The money system is going to be changed. I am surprised that your green bills that you use for exchange have not been called in as yet (to be replaced with a form of script). Martial law is to be...your national and state guards will be a factor. There will be a number system...you will have a number on your wrist. We hope and pray that none of you would have that mark put upon you. If you accept the mark, you are accepting the Mark of the Beast. The economy is putting out a false front at this moment. There is much cover up. The scales of humanity's mind must be weighted in favor of the good within the next three years or the universe will have no alternative but to cleanse the planet of negative energy. There exists right now an imbalance of energies in your world. In many ways it is darkness taking its last stand. The choice has been made. Place these words within your consciousness...there will be a day when you remember these words and realize they are given to you by the universe, and that within their energy is the strength to take the next step. (The words are)...LIGHT WILL PREVAIL! There will come a day when it may appear that darkness will extinguish the light. Do not ever allow yourself to doubt.

Sample of newspaper, magazine and newsletter reports supporting the channeled information.

Regarding Nature: December 26, 1984 (AP)—"The World Future Society...has taken stock of some recent forecasts...considered by the 30,000 member, non-profit society as the most thought-provoking of those made by scientists, scholars, and others who belong to the group. (Included are)...animal and plant species may be disappearing at the rate of 10,000 a year by 1990, with one species becoming extinct each hour. The thinning out of species is largely due to the destruction of tropical forests. (Also)...soil erosion is a worrisome agricultural problem."

We are all familiar with the extreme drought and famine in Ethiopia—and before 1985 was half over, some of the most savage storms in recent history were reported from various points on the globe, including the mass flooding in Bangladesh and China, the major earthquake in Chile, and the tornado disaster that hit Pennsylvania, Ohio, New York, and southern Canada.

Regarding Fires—From Lighting and Arson: July 11, 1985 (New York Times Service)—"The largest force of firefighters in the nation's history has been deployed to battle fast-moving brush and timber fires throughout the West, federal officials said. In the last 11 days, the fires have swept over more than 1 million acres and destroyed at least 170 homes...there have already been twice as many fires as there were in all of 1984. 'We now have the largest mobilization of manpower against wildfires that we have ever had, not just in the 20-year history of the Interagency Fire Center, but ever, and the fire season has just gotten started,' said Fire Center official William Bishop. As hundreds of blazes continued to advance in 11 Western states, fire officials attributed the widespread outbreaks to several factors: electrical storms out of Mexico that bring lightning but little rain, two years of dry weather in much of the West, and unrelenting heat. In California, however, arson is believed to have been responsible for some of the costliest blazes...arson is blamed for an unchecked fire that roared through thousands of acres of brushland and redwood groves in northern California. Major fires were being fought in Arizona, California, Idaho, Nebraska, Nevada, New Mexico, Montana, Oregon, South Dakota, Utah, and Washington. Blazes also raged in several forests of British Columbia and Alberta, Canada."

Regarding the Economy: The Sept./Oct. 1984 issue of **The Woodrew Update**[1] reports that "The debt structure, both in the U.S. and around the world, could be the trigger that provokes a massive revision of the international monetary system. The world's present total of between $600 and $700 **trillion** in dollar-denominated debt requires $600 to $700 **billion** in new money (at a 10% annual rate of interest) just to pay the interest. The $1.5 trillion in U.S. funded debt alone will require $150 billion or more in new money for interest payments. Today's circumstances are almost identical to those of 1929 except that another dimension has been added to the problem: the massive, persistent and escalating deficit financing of the welfare-warfare state."

An article in the July 15, 1985 edition of **Time** adds: "This spring the U.S. became a debtor nation for the first time since 1917...the country's net foreign debt could grow to $1 trillion by 1990. But the debt that worries economists most is the federal budget deficit. It threatens to grow at the staggering annual rate of $200 billion for the rest of the decade. Attempts to slow down the borrowing seem futile."

Regarding Martial Law: Sept. 25, 1984, Austin American Statesman—"A Defense Department plan for a network of state defense forces has been drafted as a bill Pentagon officials hope will be introduced in Congress next year. The proposed legislation will reorganize state guard units, which are separate from the National Guard, into a network of volunteer militias under control of the governors of all 50 states and three territories."

October 9, 1984—Jack Anderson's syndicated column revealed plans for martial law in the United States by the Federal Emergency Military Administration.

Three particular books add to the scenario

Collapse & Comeback[2] (1983 edition), compiled by George W. Meek. In referring to his booklet, Meek writes: "Messages channeled during the last 25 years through some of the world's most spiritually sensitive psychics have sounded a clear warning: time has almost run out for modern man. Man's economic, political and social structures will come tumbling down—and the planet itself will be subjected to cataclysmic changes which will be far more severe than the flood in Noah's time UNLESS man immediately uses his God-given ability of self determination to correct the failures."

Greta Woodrew's fascinating book — *On a Slide of Light*[3] — deals with channeled messages from extraterrestrials following the same theme. After revealing some of the tape-recorded transcripts of her conversations with these beings, who have come as friends to our planet, Greta says: "It is important to recognize the new ways of life which will open up to us, but it is also important not to let our stability be shaken in the transition. We need to learn the new rules as the time approaches. When it does come, we must stand firmly rooted, able to bend like the willow and come up with ease and grace. Each individual must be like a tree: flexible and bending to the storms of change without breaking; balanced, centered, and understanding of Nature's plan."

For the "hard facts" from the scientific viewpoint you will want to read *The Survival of Civilization*[4] — selected papers by John D. Hamaker — annotations, supporting evidence by Donald A. Weaver. Hamaker writes in the Preface: "This collection of papers was not written to please anyone. It was written as a search for truths upon which a peaceful and successful world civilization can be based. The broad truth is that without radical and immediate reform (particularly in this nation), civilization will be wrecked by 1990 and extinct by 1995. I resent the fact that my two children and three grandchildren have no future. If there are enough people who feel the same way, then perhaps we can effect our survival and establish a far better future for civilization than it has yet known." The book goes into detail on such topics as Food, Energy and Survival; Worldwide Starvation; the Role of CO_2 in the Process of Glaciation; the Glacial Process and the End of Food Supply; and Taxes, Freedom and the Constitution. It quotes a United Nations Report that estimates that by the year 2000, 90% of the agricultural land and two-thirds of the forests will be destroyed in the tropics.

A cassette tape sent from Alaska talks about the coming transition

The tape — sent to us by a Quartus member — is the recording of a lecture given by Consuela Newton in 1981. Considered a prophet of our time, Consuela says that prophecy — peeking into the past, present and future — is simply a mind technique where an individual harnesses his mind energy into a very narrow train and then directs it into the time continuum (the etheric library of Akashic Records) to look into everything that is written there. In the early 1970's she was told that 1986 is the year of no return, that man must make up his mind to elevate himself. By 1987 it will be too late, for the cause must go forward and into the effect. . . everything will be moved forward after 1986.

Consuela also looked at the ancient Mayan prophecies and found that we are in the final cycle of the fourth age of five ages that they predicted, and that we are in the final cycle of negativity. The Mayan's said that "by 1987, we would know the true face of the Lord of death and evil, and he will be revealed to us."

In reviewing the Hopi predictions, she discovered that the period of 1980 to 2000 was the time that man must choose to change himself and reach for higher ideas, higher spiritual living, or he would self-destruct. They predicted that in this period the world will purge itself clean. How dreadful this will be is up to man and his actions beforehand.

Consuela says that "a prophecy is no good unless some action can be taken. In 1986 and '87, man will begin to undergo changes in a cellular physical way, mental-spiritual way, emotional way. Take steps to adapt to changes. Heed your dreams — especially those clear emotional dreams where you wake up immediately and remember all day long. They are directing you. We have choices — we are free to begin setting our lives in a direction. It all depends on us. 1987 is the year when all motion of our karma, the results of our actions, will move forward and there will be no turning around after the end of 1986."

We've seen a few glimpses of the scenario. Now let's get practical and do something about it.

First of all, know that we *can* change the prophecies of the future. In fact, I feel that I was shown the result of our efforts in February 1985, during a group rebirthing session in the mountains of northern Georgia. I was taken back to just before this incarnation—then carried into the future where I experienced the most beautiful vision of my entire life. There seemed to be millions (billions?) of us, all moving up the side of a mountain, each carrying a lighted candle in our right hand. There was no effort in climbing the mountain... it was as though we were on level ground, yet there was the sensation of moving up. At one point I looked up and back—and as far as I could see in both directions were men, women and children, and the fire from those individual candles seemed to illumine the world with dazzling light. As we all reached the top, a beautiful Light Being in the form of a woman raised her arms and spoke these words: "The planet is healed." I simply cannot describe the emotion that I felt at that moment.

Yes, we can change the future. We can transmute the destructive energy of earthquakes, volcanic activity, tidal waves, fires, tornados and super storms. We can protect the tropical forests, remineralize the soil, eliminate hunger, and cleanse our air and water. We can segue into a new and more stable economic system without bankrupting the Treasury. We can prevent any form of repression and insure individual freedom. We can and we will heal and harmonize this planet!

How are we going to do all of this? The answer is in the first line of Jill Jackson-Miller's song—"Let There Be Peace On Earth and Let It Begin With Me." It all begins with individual you and me. Every thought we think, every feeling we have, every word we speak goes out into the atmosphere to either heal or harm. Let's be healers. Let's be harmless. Let's work joyfully moment by moment, hour by hour, day by day to uplift consciousness—to take on the Christ Vibration and release the energies of love, peace, and wholeness to harmonize our hearts and minds, our bodies, our immediate environment, our city, our nation, our world.

Our brothers and sisters from the civilizations of the stars, the Masters of Wisdom, the guardian angels, and the devas of all the kingdoms are all joyfully anticipating the penetrative thrust, the breakthrough, of Light into the race consciousness. As we have seen, that massive illumination will be made up of *individual* lights. So isn't it time now for all of us to get turned on? We *are* Spiritual Pragmatists—which means that we seek spiritually practical approaches to meeting our personal challenges and solving the problems of the planet. Recall Asher's question: "What could be more practical for an individual than to raise his consciousness to where he is living above the level of any difficulty?" That's the objective of the remaining chapters in this book.

And he also asked: "What could be more practical for the planet than for the individual to share that purer energy for the good of all?" That's why we want at least 50-million people meditating simultaneously all over the world on December 31, 1986. But we don't start or stop there. We ask you to begin participating in the World Healing Meditation this very day. Let your Light shine *now* for the benefit of every life form on this planet. Through our daily meditations beginning *now*, we can set the stage, condition the collective consciousness, and gather the Power for the mighty thrust of Spiritual Energy at noon Greenwich time on December 31, 1986. Also please do whatever you can to spread the word in and beyond New Age circles. We want to reach everyone who desires peace, wholeness and harmony in this world, and who will join us in the Mind-Link daily and on the final day of December 1986.

And then...at the same time on the last day of each month, beginning in January 1987 and each month thereafter until the race consciousness is fully Christed, let's repeat the performance. Let's continue with massive outpourings of Light and Love right through the Construction and Consolidation stages—right up to the moment of Inauguration, where the final sense of separation will be healed.

Postscript

Something very strange and extraordinary happened today and I want to share it with you. It's Sunday, July 14, 1985, and I've been reviewing this chapter for final editing. When I finished the last page I paused for a moment to reflect on Asher's concept of changing the mass and velocity of the negative energy from a rock to a feather—providing there is greater unity of purpose and participation on a world-wide basis. And it was during that contemplation that something caught my eye. I had walked around my study all morning and it hadn't been there. But now, on the floor a couple of feet to the left of my chair, I saw it...the sign, the symbol. I felt electrified—I'm simply not used to materializations of this nature. I leaned over and picked it up...a feather...gray, nearly three inches long, a little tattered on edges. I walked out and showed the feather to Jan, explaining what had happened. She said, "Oh my God." And again, there were those tears of joy.

Later we tried to apply "logic" to the experience, but there were absolutely no clues or possibilities that we could think of to explain the feather's sudden appearance. Finally, we accepted once again that Spirit had simply given us a "sign" that the Light **will** prevail!

And yes, that priceless feather is being preserved and protected as a constant reminder.

2

First Things First

I once visited with a man who talked to me about his challenges and all the steps that he had taken to demonstrate Truth in his life and affairs. And in over an hour I did not hear him refer to God, Christ, Divine Mind, Spirit, Infinite Intelligence, Father, Higher Self, or any other term above the level of the lower physical plane man.

This was not the first time that I've noticed this omission. In fact, I have found that many New Agers who have escaped from the concept of the divine finger pointing at them still felt a bit inhibited in using words referring to God. That's like the sunlight forgetting its origin, or the wave feeling funny about the ocean. While it is true that a word can never express or define God, it is also true that we cannot enjoy lasting wellness, abundance, creative self-expression, and wonderful freedom and fulfillment without a conscious relationship with our Source and a recognition of our true Identity. Just being aware of the power of the subconscious mind is not enough. We must go beyond our third-dimensional memory banks and focus on that Something within each one of us—our divine Wholeness and spiritual Reality. We are more than a black box in the solar plexus that draws in some universal power to produce miracles. We are the Power! We are the miracle!

The analogy of the sun

Imagine yourself in an old barn with a hole in the roof. It's a beautiful sunny day and you see the ray of light, a beam of the sun, pouring through the hole and focusing itself securely on the ground. What do you call the light? "It's the sun," you say. Yes! It's the sun individualized and appearing as a beam of light, forever one with its source and eternally expressing all of the attributes of the whole. In this analogy, you are the sunbeam, God is the sun. Now consider the idea that this shaft of light is conscious of itself — and of its source. But also imagine that at the point where the beam becomes grounded, there is a change in the light's vibration and the consciousness of the source is lost. If the earthbound ray does not know its origin, how can it know itself? Its focus is totally downward, so it cannot look up and trace its being to the cause of its existence. It sees itself only as a circle of light that slowly dims and dies, literally vanishing into darkness after a period of time.

But wait! Somehow the circle hears about the Truth of its being. It learns that it is not just grounded light. It is the light of its source. It is the solar energy of the sun, the very radiation from on high! This is all so new, so strange, and the circle of light begins to contemplate these ideas. Then one day its grounded vibration changes ever so slightly and it senses a higher consciousness right where it is. And the more it listens and keeps its mind stayed on that higher illumination, the more the vibration changes. In time, it becomes aware of the pillar of light that extends back from the grounded circle and it no longer believes that it is only an earthbound ray, separate and alone. As the realization deepens, the consciousness is lifted to a higher vibration and the circle of light begins to intuitively understand and know with all of its being that there is a source of light called the sun — the one presence and power of its being.

The awakening process has begun, and in the early stages of this newly-developed consciousness, the circle is heard to say, "It is the sun that does the work...I can of my own self do nothing ..my light is not mine but of the sun. . . if I speak of myself I speak a lie." But as the old identity is put away and the Truth has dawned in all its glory, we hear a new voice and a new message:

"He that sees me sees the sun. I and the sun are one, and all that the sun is, I AM. I AM the sun, for I am the shining essence of the sun. I AM the sun, for I am the warmth of the sun. I AM the sun, for I am the power of the sun. I AM the sun, for I am the radiant energy of the sun. I AM the sun, for I am the light of the world."

You, too, are more than grounded energy.

You are the Light of the world! And as you take your gaze off the appearances and change your focus to a point within, you will see the Light that you are and feel the vibration of your magnificent Self. This is the shining Essence of God, the Love of God, the Power of God, the radiant Energy of God, the Christ Self that you are in Truth. It is called the Christ because it is the Son of God. It is called the Son of God because it is the offspring, the expression — or pressing out — of the Infinite Mind of the Creator. Call it what you will, but know that it is the Reality of YOU representing the Wholeness and Completeness of God.

You are here in this incarnation for only one purpose: to heal the sense of separation and awaken to your true Identity, and to do this, you must put first things first. Everything else should be in second place and on down the line from your Number One priority of realizing the Spirit of God within you — your Spirit — your Identity. Remember, until you know your Self you will not know God!

How do you embody the Truth of your Being? Through the right use of affirmations, spiritual treatments and meditation...by making the definite decision to live the spiritual life each and every day...by remembering how to be a co-creator with God...and by being more involved with spiritual groups.

Affirmations, spiritual treatments, and meditation

I like to think of these three tools in this manner:

Affirmations — the instrument for *correcting*.

Treatments — the instrument for *conditioning*.

Meditation — the instrument for *consolidating*.

Let's take a closer look at each one.

You use affirmations like the corrector key on the typewriter, i.e. you replace error with truth. If you feel apprehensive and fearful, you remind yourself that "I am strong, powerful and fearless." If a physical ailment tries to flag your attention, deny the appearance and remember that "My body is the expression of a Divine Idea and I am whole and in perfect health." Jan calls affirmations "divine zappers" which can be used to quickly eliminate a negative train of thought. But we have to be so careful what we say because even a so-called "Truth" affirmation can continue to maintain that sense of separation in consciousness. For example, if an affirmation makes you think of you *and* God, then you have fallen back into the trap of praying to an outside God.

Now I realize that sometimes it is difficult to identify yourself with the Infinite Presence when you're wallowing in the pig pen, but we must understand that the Prodigal Son realized the Father (and His house) to be the Reality of his being. In other words, the journey home was an inside trip — an elevation of consciousness up into the spiritual realm right within his own energy field where rings and robes and fatted calves and all the other blessings are found. So we must never forget to think of God, Christ, Spirit, Father, Divine Mind — or whatever words we use — as the "Inside of the outside."

This is why we like to write our own affirmations, rather than reading something that someone else has written, and we suggest that you do the same. To give you another example, instead of saying "God is prospering me now" — we would affirm *"The Spirit of God within me, my very Christ Self, is appearing as my abundant supply now!"* And, rather than saying "It is the Father's good pleasure to give me the kingdom" — we would affirm *"My God-Self has given me the kingdom and I am enjoying the fullness of it now!"* The key is to make sure that your affirmative prayers emphasize oneness with God, rather than separateness.

Spiritual treatments. The same principle holds true in your treatments, and that's why the first step in the Manifestation Process (as a treatment example) is to identify and tune into your spiritual nature. Unless you do this, you will be working out of lower mind and lower power, and you will wonder why your outer world seems to be cast in concrete.

Also, when you are engaged in a treatment, be sure that your mind-set is not on the frequency of trying to *make* something happen. That will short-circuit the whole process. Remember that the purpose of a treatment is to *condition* your consciousness—to change the vibratory rate of your energy field—so that you may become more transparent for the activity of Spirit. Referring to the Manifestation Process again, recall that the second step is *choosing* that which you desire. Since you already have everything you could possibly desire (the spiritual prototype of all form and experience), all you are doing is deciding what you wish to express. And your *acceptance* is simply the "pulling in" of the spiritual equivalent into your subjective nature so that you can register a sense of *have* in consciousness, thus replacing a feeling of need. Then, with controlled mental picturing *(visualization)*, you are clearing the path of all obstacles and obstructions and providing an open channel for Spirit. *Loving* what you see in your mind's eye increases the energy vibration and literally propels substance to move into your world to become form and experience. Then you *speak the word* to acknowledge that you have completed your part of the treatment sequence (it is done!), and you *surrender* to the Good Will of God with a *grateful heart*. The final step is to move out into *action*, following your intuition and the promptings of your heart.

What does a treatment have to do with realizing your Identity? When you "treat" your consciousness to release your good, the results prove to you that you are one with the Creative Energy of the universe—that you have the power to heal and harmonize conditions in your world. As I have said, "Your power is only a theory until it is demonstrated." And once you have the conclusive evidence, the idea that you are just a pawn of fate will never again be dominate in your consciousness.

Meditation. The basic purpose of meditation is to become so conscious of the inner Presence that you move into the spiritual realm and take on the Christ Vibration. We are going to devote an entire chapter to this subject, but for the moment let me emphasize this point: In meditation we move into a higher consciousness where we unify (consolidate, unite, fuse) our mind with the Mind of Spirit, and it is during those moments in the Silence that we receive answers to questions, solutions to problems, and true spiritual understanding. Without this Divine Inflow, we will continue to live on the plane of the lower self as a victim of circumstances.

Making the decision to live the spiritual life

Sometimes we get so caught up in the illusions of the outer world that we forget why we are here. Our primary purpose is *not* to make money, be successful, have great friends and loving relationships, experience perfect health, and enjoy great harmony and happiness. No, these are all by-products of something else. As I said before, the real reason we are living on the earth plane is to heal the sense of separation and realize our true Identity. Then everything else follows...lavish abundance, wonderful true place success, ideal relationships, radiant health, and joyful living. In fact, the very moment we put "first things first" and make the decision to establish a spiritual life as the top priority, things begin to change—and the greater the change in consciousness, the greater the change in the outer world. As above, so below. As within, so without.

What does it mean to live the spiritual life? It doesn't necessarily mean being "religious." There is a difference between the two, you know. Spirituality is the quality of oneness with spirit, a divine reality, while religion is a man-made institutionalized system of attitudes and beliefs about God that sometimes fosters the sense of separation. Living the spiritual life means to work daily with affirmations, treatments and meditation to reorient consciousness in towards Center. It means taking control of our thoughts, words and emotions — doing whatever we have to do to work through negativity and depression. And if this calls for singing to the moon, talking to the flowers, or marching through the house beating pots and pans, then do it! Sometimes we've got to get a little crazy to blow away the negative energy, but it will be worth the effort. Some of the "Truth Students" we meet are so serious! And you know what? A deadly "serious" consciousness will be outpictured in your life as serious events, serious circumstances and serious experiences. Not necessarily bad — just serious. So lighten up. Giggle a little. Put more fun into your life. Being on the spiritual path does not mean having a heavy heart and walking through quicksand with a sinking feeling. It means being joyful, cheerful, gleeful, buoyant, jubilant, glad, lighthearted.

Living the spiritual life also means putting more into life than you're taking out, which means to do the best you can wherever you are, to help others at every opportunity, and to radiate love and peace in every situation. Above all, it means to practice the Presence of God throughout each day. . . in other words, think about, contemplate, love, adore, ponder on and dwell upon your Christ Self!

Remembering how to be a co-creator

You provide the lamp for the light, the channel for the expression, the vehicle for the manifestation — and God does the rest. As has been said so many times: the Power can work *for* you only as it can work *through* you. So what is your role in the scheme of things? To maintain a consciousness of one accord with the Spiritual Self — to agree with the Principles of the Higher Vibration. And what are these principles? They are abundance, wellness, harmony, and divine order. When you are in agreement with this kind of spiritual Thinking, you become the channel for the expression of these Divine Ideas.

Let me give you another example. Your God-Self thinks only thoughts of abundance and never lack or limitation.

These thoughts are in the form of pure energy within the Mind of your Higher Self. This thought energy constitutes a momentous force, a power, a mighty thrust which presses out and radiates through your consciousness. This Thought Energy — this Mind Power — is pregnant with the thinkingness of unlimited supply, boundless prosperity, overflowing abundance. As this copious substance moves through your consciousness, it is either distributed "as is" — or altered according to the vibration of your energy field. It lets itself be impressed with the "shape" of your consciousness, and then goes forth into the physical world to become, or appear as, forms and experiences relating to your concept of abundance. Your financial supply is simply an outpicturing of your consciousness. And the same principle applies whether it is health, harmonious relationships, success, or anything else in your world.

To be a co-creator with the Presence and Power within, you must learn once again how to cooperate with Spirit. And one of the best ways that I have found in working with the Law is to remember that my God-Self is always thinking perfect thoughts, and that anything I could possibly desire in the outer world is already included in that Thought Energy. Now, since this impregnated creative energy radiates from the center to the circumference of my being, it means that there is no time or place when I do not have total fulfillment in any particular area of my life. But I must constantly be aware of this Truth!

Using the prosperity example again, with this kind of awareness you can say "I am abundance" with total certainty because the energy of abundance is yours. *It is you!* It flows from your Higher Self, so it is yours. *It is you!* It flows through your consciousness, so it is yours. *It is you!* And it goes before you to create new forms and conditions in your life, which become *yours* to use, enjoy and share. You are abundance through and through — within and without — above and below. When you condition your consciousness to this Truth, you will be rich in mind *and* manifestation as a co-creator with God.

Your involvement with spiritual groups

"Where two or three are gathered together in my name, there am I in the midst of them." Think about that statement. When only two or three gather together in the Christ Vibration, in the spiritual energy of Love, then the fullness of Spirit is there with all its Power, Vision, and Creativeness. When just two or three come together to share in Love and Light, all of the attributes of spiritual mastery are there, too — total faith, perfect understanding, great enthusiasm, divine wisdom, infinite love, boundless joy, spiritual strength, total forgiveness, and the pure Life Force of God. And yes, when just a couple meet in uplifted consciousness to behold the Christ within, the very presence of Jesus is there, releasing his light to dispel the darkness.

This is why it is so important for all of us to share our time with other spiritually minded people. When we come together in a church, for example, we are literally focusing the incredible energy and awesome power of the universe right in the sanctuary. We are not there to just listen to someone standing at the pulpit; we are not there to relax for an hour and then go home feeling pink and fuzzy all over. No, we are there to share God!

I also feel that it is important to gather in small groups for master-minding and study on a regular basis. When you work together spiritually in groups, you cannot think healing and harmonious thoughts for yourself without benefiting everyone else. Each soul can be lifted into a new level of consciousness where all good things are indeed possible.

Now I am not saying that you should spend less time in private meditation and spiritual study. I am suggesting that you *supplement* your personal activities with group involvement as a way of expanding your consciousness. If you will do this while disciplining yourself to live the spiritual life and remembering to co-create with God at every opportunity, you'll find your spiritual evolution taking quantum leaps.

3

God Meets You Where
You Are

The power of God meets us on whatever level of consciousness we may be experiencing at the time. Think about that.
Perhaps another way of saying the same thing is that our
world is always a reflection of how we think and feel. That's
the way the Law works. To give you a clearer understanding of
the principle involved, we'll look at a few illustrations.

Let's say that you are a pure materialist and the only priority in your life is a material or physical goal. Whether it is to
earn a certain sum of money, land a job, reach the top rung of
the corporate ladder, find a mate, or to have "security" in
later years, your entire focus is on the planning and the
implementation of the plan to achieve the goal. There must
always be a third-dimensional "target" to shoot at, and the
target will marshall the physical-mental forces of consciousness and direct your energy toward that desire fulfillment.

Does God work with you on this level? Certainly! But the
power will work with you, and for you, only as it works *as* you. In
other words, if meeting your objectives on this level requires that
you ignore everything else in life and become a workaholic, then
the power working *as* your consciousness will assume that role and
you will burn a lot of midnight oil. With the one-pointed focus
of the goal/objective in mind, you will acquire all the know-how
you can; you'll learn all the techniques in "playing to win;" and

you'll work with personal will power to achieve your goal regard-less of the consequences.

You will learn how to cope with fear through aggressive action, and your self-image will develop into a mental picture of yourself as a shrewd, tough, decisive go-getter. And while stress and tension may affect the physical system, there are always good doctors to fix you up and send you back on the road to success. If a marriage dissolves through the tunnel vision of this type of consciousness, so be it. There are always others out there who will appreciate you.

Yes, the impersonal power of God does meet you on this level, appearing as the dedication required to achieve the goal, the stamina to stay with it, the medicine to ease your pain, and the attracting force to bring people into your life with a similar vibration in consciousness—positive or nega-tive. What about heart-felt prayers? A fervent, persistent prayer spoken from this consciousness is always answered, with the fullness of the deliverance dependent upon the mea-sure of "blind" faith set in motion. "It is done unto you as you believe."

I don't want to give the impression that people on this level cannot be happy. They can, but their happiness is usu-ally measured by how close they are to achieving their goals, and the carrot must forever be on the end of the stick.

The discovery of the genie

As the materialist achieves one goal after another (or seem-ingly so) and sets up new targets, new objectives, there may come a time when a sense of dissatisfaction creeps into con-sciousness and the questions start. "What is all this for?" "Why isn't there more happiness in my life?" What can I do to find greater peace of mind?" After a while this nagging feeling may lead the person to the discovery of Truth ideas...perhaps from a book, or through the sharing of another individual. The intellectual interest is stirred, and the exciting mystery of the subconscious mind begins to cap-ture his imagination. He reads or hears that affirmations can "make things happen" and much emphasis is placed on mind power. The holy servant has been found, and the individual is determined to use this servant to find the missing peace and happiness. After all, when you've found the secret of mind over matter, you can let the genie of the mind do the work. But genies can also make you think that you are more evolved than you are. Let me give you an example.

Emmet Fox wrote about a young child who had just fallen off a bridge into the water below. He pointed out that if you are spiritually evolved, you can just stand there on the bridge and "see" the child safely on the shore, and lo and behold, the child *is* safely on shore. But if you are not in an evolved state of consciousness, you don't stand around waiting for something to happen. Fox suggests that you quickly dive off the bridge into the water—praying all the way—and save the child.

I have found that many of the "third dimensionals" who are introduced to New Thought try to demonstrate while still operating out of lower mind and power, and the result is a lot of "drowning." One man I know would certainly match the description of a wheeler-dealer. When he discovered metaphysics he decided that "make-it-happen" affirmations would unleash the genie to wheel and deal for him and he wouldn't have to work so hard. His demonstration was the loss of his job. He had been out of work for about six months (and affirming daily that a new position was being attracted to him) when he called me. The gist of the conversation was that his prayers were not working and he needed some help. After a few minutes I asked, "Why don't you go find a job?" And he replied, "Because I want to do it God's way." (To him, "God" was simply a force in his subconscious that was amenable to control by the power of suggestion.) After discussing the concept of the one Presence and Power universal and individualized, I said something along these lines: "God always meets us on the level of our consciousness. You are out of work and you want a job. Right now God sees you as totally fulfilled and enjoying creative self-expression in your true place, but the vibration of your consciousness is not strong enough for this Divine Ideal to express perfectly. So while you're continuing to work to uplift and expand consciousness, go out and look for a job, affirming all the time that God is with you, directing your every move." He followed these instructions and quickly found an excellent job.

Just remember that when your consciousness is more material than spiritual, you may find your answer through specific activity on the material plane, i.e. diving off the bridge, reviewing the want ads, working with the law of averages in making sales calls, etc. And as you combine these physical-mental activities with spiritual work to expand consciousness, you will find your feeling nature coming into play.

Emotions become the fuel for the next phase of consciousness

When Jan and I first discovered Truth concepts, we were living in the Chicago area in the 1960's. We had been functioning in a "physical-mental" consciousness most of our lives, but when we were exposed to Truth, it didn't take long to activate our emotional system. Perhaps it was the excitement and enthusiasm we felt...it was as though we had always known the metaphysical principles, and the "remembering" was a great stimulus to our feeling nature.

We soon made a list of twenty things, experiences and conditions we wanted and we went to work. We began every morning by reviewing our list, imagined that we had the fulfillment of each desire, affirmed that it was so, and spoke the word that it was done. And soon everything on that list came to pass—and so we made new and bigger and better lists, with demonstrations following. But before we could completely conquer our world, everything fell apart like a sawdust doll.

We realized later that we had been operating strictly on mind power (conscious/subconscious), and I can assure you that there is a missing ingredient when you are working only with third dimensional forces. Even though we had united the mental, emotional and physical energies, we were still operating on the plane of the lower self, or personality. We had not yet tuned into that Christ Vibration within, the

Super-consciousness. We forgot Jesus' instructions to seek the kingdom **first.**

You may ask, "Did God meet you on that integrated level of personality consciousness?" Yes indeed! As we began to choose exactly what we wanted in life and developed the consciousness for those choices, they appeared in our lives. But here was the snag: we were developing a consciousness of things, material conditions and physical experiences, rather than a consciousness of God. And the things, conditions and experiences were only as permanent in the outer world as our ability to constantly **project** them. It was like having a tire with a slow leak...we constantly had to pump it up. In essence, the new "world" that we had projected for ourselves required constant attention and mind-management through affirmations and treatments, and day after day our attention was placed on drilling the mind and programming consciousness. We felt that we couldn't leave the "projection booth" for one moment, but obviously we did — and the screen went blank. We just couldn't hold the picture anymore, but in the divine scheme of things, that was the best thing that ever happened to us because it forced us to surrender and let everything go.

Becoming spiritually centered

When you're back at the bottom of the mountain, there is only one place to go and that's up — and so we started the climb again, this time with a total dedication to the Spirit within. And as we began to reshape and retune consciousness, we were very gently led by Spirit to redirect the focus of our affirmations, treatments and meditations. Whereas before we had been affirming, treating and meditating to demonstrate a better "outer" condition, we began to use these tools to demonstrate the Love and Power of God. I'm not saying that we no longer had any desires, plans or visions of a totally fulfilled life. Not hardly. In fact, the scenario of our Life Plan expanded even more as we glimpsed what was included in the Father's storehouse. But there was a total redirection in our spiritual work.

For example, all former prosperity treatments were directed to the phenomenal world, as if to *make* more money appear in the bank, or create conditions whereby new clients would appear and new cars and houses would manifest. Health treatments were directed to the body, relationship treatments were aimed at the particular individuals, and protection treatments were focused on unseen negative forces "out there" somewhere. The whole focus of mind and emotions was *outer* directed.

Then one day, without really realizing what we were doing, we began to affirm, treat and meditate for the sole purpose of awakening consciousness. We were becoming spiritually centered, and with this change in direction came the knowledge that the only Real and lasting demonstration is the demonstration of the Truth of Being. So instead of constantly affirming prosperity, we began to affirm our oneness with the Source of Abundance right within us that has no conception whatsoever of lack. And in our spiritual treatments, we began by tuning into the Christ Vibration **first** and continued from the standpoint that it was our Christ Self doing the treating—and since Spirit knows only life, love, order, harmony, perfection and nothing to the contrary, no obstacles or barriers loomed up to block our vision. And in our meditations we devoted our time to contemplating the Christ Presence, the indwelling Spirit, knowing that this True Self would awaken the subconscious from within—rather than it being programmed from without.

Things didn't completely turn around overnight, but as the changes began to occur, even the small ones were very meaningful. And soon the momentum picked up and our lives began to change dramatically with greater prosperity, beautiful health, and more loving relationships than we had ever known. You see, when God meets you on the **spiritual** level of consciousness, it's the Real Thing. The "effect" is lasting, the fulfillment is joyous, and there is the constant emotion of gratitude.

As I said in *The Superbeings*, "I'm not home yet"—but I know that there is nothing more important in my life now than realizing, totally and completely, the Presence of God. Truly, that is the Secret of Life and the Key to Mastery.

A few realizations along the way

• Prayer is the opening of consciousness to God and providing a door for Spirit to enter the third-dimensional plane. While God is omnipresent, the activity of God cannot take place in your experience except through a spiritual consciousness.

• "I and the Father are one." That is true in the absolute, but it is not true in your experience until you realize it.

• Prayer is not trying to convince God to do something for you. It is becoming aware of the Presence within you, knowing that God acts for your highest good *through* this conscious awareness.

• The Father has given you the kingdom. It's already yours, and everything you could possibly desire in life is in the kingdom. When you love enough, the kingdom radiates out through the door that love has opened.

• Abundance is yours now. You would not be alive in this world if this were not true. The life force and the energy of supply are the same. Recognize your Source and let the living abundance pour forth into your experience.

• Disease, illness and ailments are effects, simply "appearances." If you judge such an appearance as bad, you bind it in your experience. Withhold judgement and let the Presence correct the appearance.

• There is nothing that your Christ Self cannot do for you. In fact, It is doing everything for you now. Relax.

• You don't "own" anything. Everything is an expression and extension of the Presence within you, so all belongs to Spirit. Remember, "the earth is the Lord's, and the fullness thereof."

• Whatever you resist you give energy to. Whatever you give energy to continues to be a part of your experience. If you want a so-called evil out of your life, stop resisting it. When you pull the plug on its power, it dies out of your experience.

- If you believe in good and evil, you have created a second power out of your own energy, and you will experience that evil because it is in your consciousness. When you realize Omnipotence, the one and only Power, then only the Power of Good is at work in your life.
- Don't put your faith in anything visible, either "good" or "evil." That which appears good may not be, and to fear an evil (put your faith in it) will only sustain it. Place your faith only in the Invisible Presence and Power within you.
- You don't need to tell others how spiritual you are. They already know "by your fruits." Your health, harmony, peace, joy and fulfillment are in direct proportion to the level of your spirituality.
- You are not here to live a passive life. The Universe needs you.
- The only problem facing you in life is the belief in separation from your Source. Solve that one and all the others will vanish.
- Before you look for "new" Truths, put into practice those you already know.
- Everyone in your life is there by the Law of Attraction. And whether you consider them good, bad or indifferent, they are there to help you experience your self.
- If you feel a negative emotion about a personality characteristic in another person, chances are you have that same flaw in your consciousness, otherwise you could not see it in others.

4

Mastery Through Meditation

If you've ever asked anyone to define meditation, you may be just as confused as you were before you asked because it means different things to different people. Our objective in this chapter is to clear up some of the confusion and discuss the practical aspects of this marvelous tool for expanding consciousness.

Meditation benefits

Meditation will alleviate stress, reduce high blood pressure, increase resistance to disease, increase the autonomic stability of the nervous system, improve the power of concentration, tap deep reserves of intelligence, contribute to mental clarity, stabilize emotions, improve human relations, relieve insomnia, improve coordination of mind and body, increase learning ability, and boost creativity. Numerous medical and academic studies have revealed such evidence. But of even greater importance are the *spiritual* benefits. Meditation is a tool that will enable you to make contact with your spiritual Self, and it is that intent that we will discuss.

Definition and use

Meditation is a relaxing of the body, a stilling of the emotions, and a narrowing of attention so that the mind may contemplate the inner Reality and move into another dimension in consciousness. There must be no effort in doing this; it must come easily and naturally. It is a gentle raising of vibrations so that one may come into alignment with the spiritual Self.

The motive for meditation must be pure with no thought of psychic experiences or making contact with "the other side." Meditation is not an instrument for emptying the mind and creating a void to attract illusionary voices from the astral plane. To do this can be dangerous. The objective must be to establish a channel between Spirit and the lower nature, resulting in an outpouring of the higher energy. And it is through this "outpouring" that you will become receptive to the "still, small voice" from within. You will also be energized spiritually so that you will have the creative power to carry out the instructions of the Higher Self, and the change in vibration in your individual energy field will be permanent. It is also important to understand that the spiritual vibration taken on during meditation becomes a positive force in the race consciousness of man, and is of great benefit to the animal, plant, and mineral kingdoms.

Speaking from personal experience, I have found the following guidelines to be helpful in moving from the busy world up into the silence.

1. Until you become proficient in the techniques, it is best to have several meditation periods of short duration during the day—10 to 20 minutes each.

2. Don't take your problems with you into meditation. Remember that your primary goal is to make contact and commune with Spirit. If you take a laundry list of grievances with you, you'll never reach the Secret Place. Furthermore, when the contact is made, you are to let Spirit do all the "talking" while you simply listen.

3. It is helpful to have a particular room and chair for those special times with Self, especially during the learning/training phase. Later you will find that you can meditate

anywhere at any time because the inward journey will have become an automatic process.

4. Begin by surrounding yourself with the White Light, and then commence your breathing exercises to relax the body and settle the mind and emotions.

5. Contemplate an object or symbol *within* consciousness (not outside), or if you're not a visualizer, use a mantra. A mantra is a word repeated over and over again to synchronize the vibrations, and may be used in conjunction with the breathing exercises. They usually have no linguistic meaning, which keeps the mind from thinking about the significance of the word. If you have a favorite mantra, use it — otherwise, you can make one up, insuring that the word has no meaning to you.

6. After a few moments of contemplating the symbol, the mind will shift to a spiritual idea, which in turn will attract other divine ideas into consciousness — finally moving beyond words and into the silence. Or, in the case of the mantra, the mind will rise above the repeated impulses of the mantra and into a higher level of consciousness.

7. Once in the "upper room" of consciousness, the objective is to listen, hear and heed the Voice within.

Over the years Jan and I have experimented with just about every form of meditation that has come to our attention, but we had to find our own key to unlock the door to the inner Chamber, just as you will have to find yours. But perhaps we can help you in your search by sharing how we use the seven points listed above.

The Oneness meditation

We both have a favorite chair in particular rooms where we do most of our meditating. Those chairs and rooms now have a certain vibration of energy in and around them, which makes "getting into" meditation much easier.

Secondly, when I sit down in the chair I tell myself that I am now going to take time from the third-dimensional world and visit my God-Self on the Fourth Dimensional plane, and that everything on earth can wait until I return. That sets the tone for the importance of the meditation period. Then I sit up straight, feet on the floor, hands resting comfortably in my lap, close my eyes, and surround myself with the White Light.

Next, I commence my breathing exercises, at first taking short, powerful breaths to release all tension and as a preparation for concentration. After a few minutes, I begin to focus attention on my breathing as I inhale, hold the breath, exhale, pause, and begin the cycle again. When my body is relaxed and my mind still, I begin to concentrate on an object that I purposely call forth in my mind, such as a golden circle of light, the warm red of the rising sun, or the fire of a candle — and I begin a period of controlling my mind (thoughts) by visualizing, focusing, concentrating, and contemplating the symbol.

As I literally move into and become one with the object of contemplation, I begin to ponder my oneness with God. Sometimes a divine Truth will come forth automatically; other times the seed must be planted. . . a seed thought such as "I and the Father are one" — or — "Christ in me, my hope of glory" — or — "Christ liveth in me." Then, as if pages are turning, other ideas or symbols are added, each revealing a truth relating to my oneness with God and my divinity, and the spiritual vibration grows stronger. After a few minutes the "pages" become blank — the words stop — and with *full alertness* I move into the silence. Here I feel as one in the very presence of God. There is stillness and quiet, and my entire consciousness is in a listening mode, and it is here that the Voice speaks. It is here that the spiritual infusion is felt. It is here that the contact is made. It is here that the soul becomes an open channel for the activity of Spirit.

What I am saying will be of little benefit to you unless you experience the meditation miracle yourself, so do what you have to do to learn the techniques — then practice, practice, practice! Practice your breathing exercises. Practice focusing and concentrating on an image in your mind — or using a mantra — to control your thoughts. Practice planting seed thoughts of Truth and watch as they give birth to higher and deeper revelations. Practice meditating on your oneness with God.

It will be well worth the effort. During and following periods of oneness with your Self you will receive answers to your questions and guidance where there had been uncertainty. Through the Contact, old error patterns will be dissolved, your consciousness will become a clear and clean center through which Spirit may work, and your world will take on new meaning as it reflects the Christ Vibration. But remember, don't try to *make* anything happen. Take the inner journey simply for the thrill of meeting your Master Self, and then let go and listen. Let go and let Spirit fulfill Itself through you! Now let's talk about another form of meditation.

The illusion to Reality meditation — also called a "meditative treatment"

Whenever my consciousness gets out of tune in a particular downward direction, I try to sit down immediately and get in touch with the Reality behind the illusion. For example, let's say that you find yourself facing a financial challenge. This means that there is a false belief in consciousness which is outpicturing itself as limitation in your world. There is simply a misconception and a misunderstanding in your mind regarding the Source of your supply and the loving Givingness of Spirit. To meet this challenge, you should "operate" (perform spiritual surgery) on your deeper-than-conscious level of mind.

Again, you would go to your meditation place, become still, relaxed and receptive through your breathing exercises. Then slowly and with feeling read a Truth statement on abundance, meditating on each word, contemplating each sentence until the true meaning registers in consciousness. Take this prosperity statement as an example:

The Spirit of God within me is the Source of my supply. My Christ Self knows only lavish abundance, and the activity of that Knowingness is constantly at work in my life and affairs. My Spirit is now appearing as my all-sufficiency.

Now let's break the statement down and focus intently on the meaning and significance of the words.

The Spirit of God (contemplate the idea behind the words "the Spirit of God" until you feel something within. Speak the words silently and watch the other thoughts that flow in to expand your thinking.)

within me (dwell on the meaning of "within me"....what does that mean? Let the idea roll around in your mind and feeling nature until you have a degree of understanding.

is the Source (what does "Source" mean? It means the cause, the authority, the well-spring, the foundation. Visualize a fountain of unlimited all-good within you. Get a feel for what it means to have a SOURCE of all you could possibly desire right within your consciousness.)

of my supply. (supply is a word encompassing the fullness of the manifestation. It means all that you could ask for. Contemplate the idea that because your supply comes forth from an unlimited Source, then the supply itself must be unlimited.)

My Christ Self knows only lavish abundance (ponder the idea that the You of you—your Higher Self—cannot conceive of lack and limitation, therefore there is no reality to insufficiency. There is no duality in that infinite Mind within you. It knows only all-sufficiency, abundance, copiousness, plentifulness, surplus. And this Consciousness of Infinite Plenty is endless, limitless, boundless, measureless.)

and the activity of that Knowingness (contemplate the action of that Super Mind within you. Generate a greater awareness of the power at work—the force, the movement, the radiation of that All-Knowing Mind filled with thoughts of lavish abundance.)

is constantly at work in my life and affairs. (Reflect on the word "constantly" and gain an understanding of what it means...unfailing, permanent, enduring. Sense the divine purpose at work; feel the very will of God, the cosmic urge to express, active in your world.)

My Spirit is now appearing as my all-sufficiency. (You are now aware of the torrent of creative-creating Energy radiating from you and going before you to manifest as the fulfillment of your desire. Think...even before the supply becomes visible, you have it. It is yours! Acknowledge this Truth with love, joy and a heart overflowing with gratitude.)

In that state of consciousness, "wait upon the Lord." Remain still. Listen. Feel. Keep your mind focused on the Presence within, and let Spirit work in and through you with perfect ease.

Now let's work with a healing meditation.

The forgiving, cleansing love of Christ now frees me from all negative thoughts and emotions. I turn within and open the door to the River of Life and let the healing currents flow through me. I am purified and vitalized by this Christ Life within. I am renewed according to the perfect pattern of Spirit. God sees me as well, whole, complete, vibrant, strong, and perfect. And so I am!

Go back and contemplate, ponder upon, each word and sentence. Meditate until you have an understanding of the ideas behind the words, and then move on to the next sentence. As your consciousness becomes in tune with this Truth, it will shift from a focus on illusion to a centering on Reality. Your consciousness of God as your health becomes your wellness, your wholeness, your perfection.

Write your own meditations and use the same procedure for healing relationships, finding the right mate, locating a job, or any other challenge you may be facing. Just keep in mind that all you're doing in the process is opening your consciousness for the activity of Spirit. You already have everything spiritually. Your objective is simply to release it.

You can also use the "meditative treatment" approach with your favorite spiritual book. Read a line or two, meditate on the

ideas behind the words until there is an inner understanding—
then read a few more lines, pause for meditation, and so on. If
you think this is too time consuming, consider the old story of the
man from India who asked an American missionary to tell him
about his religion.

The American said, "Well, it's really based on a prayer
given to us by Jesus."

"And what is this prayer?"

The missionary replied, "Our Father..." But before he
could say anything else the Indian vanished into the crowd.

A few years later he reappeared as an adept, saying: "I am
now ready for the next lesson."

Can you imagine what would happen to your consciousness if
you meditated on those two words for several years? Even a few
weeks of such contemplation could change your life!

Particular Meditative Treatments for:

Total Fulfillment

*What do I know of God? God is Life, Life is omnipresent,
all is alive. I see this in the wonders of nature. I see this in
myself. I am alive because I am Life. My Life is God's Life.
My Life is God. I feel my livingness within me. I feel
God. My awareness of God is growing.*

*God is Love. I feel Love in my heart and know that this is
the very Spirit of God flowing through my feeling nature.
I could not love without God. I love, therefore, I am one
with God. My understanding of God is growing.*

*God is Wisdom and Intelligence. God is Mind, and I sense
the Infinite Knowingness of that Mind within me. I think. I
know. And that with which I think and know is God's Mind
in expression. My knowledge of God is growing.*

*Where is God? God is where I AM. God is what I AM. I
AM an individualization of God and the Spirit of God
dwells within me, as me. I AM the Light of the world. I*

turn within to the Light and say, "Thou art the Christ, the Spirit of the Living God. You are my Spirit, my Soul, my Body. When I look at Thee I see Me." And I listen in the Silence for the acknowledgement from within.

I am now conscious of God, of my Christ Self. I AM the Christ of God, the Truth of God, the Self of God. Through this consciousness of the Reality of me, I open the door to Spirit. I draw into my mind and feeling nature the Wholeness of Spirit, the Allness of God, and my consciousness is filled with the Light of Truth.

I know now that there is nothing that I could truly desire that is not at this very moment standing at the door of my consciousness, ready to appear in my life and affairs. I have only to be conscious of this Truth and every need is met, every problem solved, every question answered. My consciousness of God within is all I will ever need for all eternity.

What is God?

God is Lavish Abundance.

I am now conscious of God within as my abundant supply.

God is Perfection, Total Wellness.

I am now conscious of God within as my radiant health.

God is Perfect Love.

I am now conscious of God within as the activity of my loving relationships.

God is Perfect Harmony.

I am now conscious of God within as the harmony of my

home and business.

God is the only Power.

I am now conscious of God within as my safety and protection.

God is the only Presence.

I am now conscious of God within as the guiding, guarding, protecting Presence watching over my loved ones.

God is Perfect Peace.

I am now conscious of God within all as total peace on earth.

My consciousness of God within as each of these experiences is the experience in my life and affairs. I am now experiencing only God in mind and manifestation.

My consciousness of God within as my total fulfillment is my fulfillment. I am now experiencing total fulfillment.

I am abundance.

I am radiant health.

I am loved and loving.

I am in perfect harmony.

I am totally protected.

I am at perfect peace.

And what I see for myself, I see for all others.

I am one with God. I am one with all. And it is so.

Realizing Self
There is but one Presence, one Life, one Power, one Cause in this universe, the Spirit of God, the Spirit of Love everywhere present.

This Presence, this Life, this Power, this Cause is individualized as me now. It is Who I am. It is What I am. I am the Allness of God, the Allness of Love in individual expression. I AM, I AM, I AM.

I look above me, below me, around me, within me, and all I see is God. God is all there is. All there is is God. GOD IS, GOD IS, GOD IS.

I am complete. I am whole. Because God is expressing as me, there is nothing missing in my life. I now release all fear and doubt and lift up my vision to behold my Self as I am in Truth.

(rest in the Silence)

Cleansing Error Patterns and Releasing Negative Energy
I enter the chamber of my consciousness and look deeply within. I examine all the thoughts, feelings, and beliefs that have been stored there for so long. As each error thought appears, I release it to the indwelling Christ and let it go.

There are those I know well should be eliminated, and then there are those that are hidden, buried deeply, for I could not quite face them. Even now I hesitate to expose them for fear of pain that they may bring, or changes I may not want to accept. Yet I have the urge to move up higher and I cannot take them with me. I will ask the Presence to go before me and lead the way.

Divine Love, please show me the barriers that hold me from my oneness with you, my beautiful Christ Self. Let your Light dissolve, even as it reveals, the errors in my consciousness. Dear God, who art within me, I am willing to surrender all that I am to you. Show me the way. I cannot do it alone. Lift me up, my Spirit, to your Consciousness, that I may see the Light and be made new and whole and free.

If I hold any one of your children in condemnation or unforgiveness, I choose to release them. I choose to give to all whom I feel obligated their due. I love them. I bless them. I wish them their highest good. I choose to withhold from no one what is theirs. I choose the very highest of your Good for all.

Show me the way to surrender my life, my body, my love, my mind, my family, my debts, my fears, my possessions, my thoughts, words and deeds to the Higher Self within. If I must let something go, take it. If I must do something, show me, tell me, direct me. Take me as I am and lift me up to your highest Vision. I hold back nothing. If I do, show me and I will hold it back no longer.

I choose to surrender. I choose to understand. I choose to believe in you and nothing else and show forth only your fruits in my expression.

At this moment I am lifted up into the Christ Consciousness where there is only Light and Love and Life.

Healing in the Light

Visualize a candle, and as you ignite the flame let it symbolize the radiant energy of Spirit within you. Contemplate the warm glow of the flame. Let its soft, sensuous, sweetness stimulate and soothe your Soul. Now meditate on these thoughts...

I SEE THE LIGHT. The Light beckons me to partake of its essence.

I MOVE INTO THE LIGHT. The Light welcomes me and fills me with its lovely luminance.

I AM ILLUMINED BY THE LIGHT. Understanding and wisdom permeate my consciousness with the knowingness of Who and What I AM. The Light of God fills and lifts me up to Superconsciousness.

I AM ONE WITH THE LIGHT. I am one with God Energy, pulsating in ever greater degrees, melting me, molding me, filling me, using me for its perfect expression.

I AM THE LIGHT. I am the Light of the World.

I RADIATE THE LIGHT. I send forth the Light. The Light seeks that which is like itself. The Light that I AM radiates out in ever increasing intensity to join all other Lights. The Lights unite to become one great, glowing, golden fire.

WE ARE THE LIGHT. Finding fullness in union, the radiance increases and expands. Moving out, filling space, the healing Light flows in and through and around this world, harmonizing, purifying, spiritualizing . . . out into the universe, into infinity.

ALL IS THE LIGHT.

THE LIGHT IS UNENDING, ETERNAL.

THE LIGHT IS GOD.

ALL IS THE LIGHT.

WE ARE THE LIGHT.

I AM THE LIGHT.

I REST IN THE LIGHT.

NOTE: The final two meditations were adapted from material written by Jan Price and previously used in Workshops and Quartus Reports.

The World Healing Meditation is included in the Appendix.

5

From Fearful to Fearless

The Tibetan Master, Djwhal Khul, has said that "fear is the dominant astral energy at this time, and sensitive humanity succumbs all too easily to it."[1]

What can we do about fear? What is the principle of freedom from fear? In the magnificent Light-filled Force Field that we are, where is the negative energy of fear located? What can we do to transmute it into the pure energy of Love?

We need to answer these questions because fear is the root cause of essentially every problem that we face on the third-dimensional plane. Many of us may not be conscious of our fears, but if we monitor our thoughts, words and actions each day we'll see that in one way or another we are constantly affirming "I am afraid . . ." Afraid of lack, abundance, failure, success, sickness, health, darkness, light, and certain foods, people, the Government, the bomb, accidents, invasions of privacy, the weather, and on and on.

I believe that the first thing we must do about fear is to recognize that there is absolutely nothing to fear. According to *A Course in Miracles*,[2] to say that there is nothing to fear "simply states a fact. It is not a fact to those who believe in illusions, but illusions are not facts. In truth, there is nothing to fear." Fear is a belief in illusions and illusions are of our own creation. Therefore, what we fear is what we ourselves project on the screen of life out of the lower vibration of the mortal ego. What is the mortal ego? Let's think of it as a faulty belief system that has attached itself to our personal I AM. It is a congregation of thoughts based on appearances, a belief in good and evil, a pool of conscious energy that believes more in the absence of God than in the Presence of God.

Why is an Awakened One *fear-less* and living the abundant life, while others are *fear-full* and living a life of insufficiency and desperation? The difference is that the focus of energy has been transferred from ego to Soul and Spirit . . . the emphasis is placed on individuality rather than personality. How was this accomplished? What did they do that we can do? One activity has been a thorough overhaul of their belief system.

Changing the vibration of the belief system

Let's pause for a moment now and look at your particular belief system. Do you believe in a Higher Power of Infinite Goodness operating in your life? If you say "yes" then your life *must* be totally fulfilled right now and you are experiencing an all-sufficiency of all good. If you say "yes" but your life is not whole and harmonious, then you are only thinking and assuming that you believe in the One Presence and Power. You see, in order to determine what you really believe—or the *degree* of your beliefs—you must look at your world because beliefs are forever externalized. Your world always mirrors your convictions.

To put it rather bluntly, if you are ill, you do not believe whole-heartedly in God as the Life of your body and your eternal Wellness. If you are suffering lack, or if you anticipate experiencing limitation in the future, you have not completely accepted the Truth that God is your Source, Substance and Supply, constantly expressing as lavish abundance. In short, if you fear anything, you do not truly believe in God.

Now let me explain what a "belief" is. A belief is a point of conscious energy pulsating to a certain vibration within the sphere of its own realm of possibility/probability. This means that there are varying *degrees* of belief, with the externalization reflecting the exact degree. Think of a rheostat controlling the light of a lamp. As you rotate the knob, there is greater illumination in the room. As you reverse the process, the room becomes darker. The light in the room is directly related to the setting of the rheostat. Now consider the idea that each belief in your overall belief system operates in similar fashion to the rheostat. When the belief is total and complete, it is outpictured in all its fullness at a level (or degree) of 100 percent. But there are also "settings" ranging backwards from 100, i.e. 90-80-70-60-50-40-30-20-10 down to zero or total unbelief.

Apply this illustration to specific areas in your life. In your financial affairs, for example, if you are in the lower ranges you are living in a state of insufficiency, which accurately reflects your belief setting. However, the higher you move up in the degree of your belief in God as your all-providing Source, the greater your financial freedom and independence will be, and fears regarding lack and limitation will vanish from your energy field.

Take a few minutes now and rate yourself on a "belief setting" of from zero to 100 in the following areas. Be totally honest with yourself and write in the number for each category. Make sure that the number you write is the one you think is correct for your present degree of belief— considering both your intuitive feelings and the appearance in your life and affairs, as related to that particular category.

Belief Category   *Rating: 0 to 100*

- I believe that God is expressing through me now as my perfect health and well-being.   _____
- I believe that God is expressing now as abundant all-sufficiency in my affairs.   _____
- I believe that God is expressing now as total safety and protection in my life.   _____
- I believe that God is expressing now as total safety and protection in the lives of my loved ones.   _____
- I believe that God is expressing now as my perfect relationship with all people.   _____
- I believe that God is expressing now as

creative fulfillment and my true place
success.   _____

- I believe that God is expressing now as
  the ideal living conditions for me and
  my family.   _____
- I believe that God is expressing now as
  complete unconditional love within my
  family and my world.   _____
- I believe that God is expressing now as
  Peace on Earth.   _____

Let's look again at our objectives. First of all, we want to banish
fear from our lives, knowing that fear is an energy block prevent-
ing the total expression of the One Power and Presence. The negative energy of fear is the result of error thoughts developed in a
belief system that denies Omnipresence, Omnipotence and
Omniscience. Therefore, we must restructure our beliefs and
change the "dial set" from degrees of partial belief to the full
radiance of absolute conviction. In essence, we want to believe
totally and completely in God, knowing that through this total
and maximal knowingness, Spirit will literally reveal conditions
that can only be called "heavenly" for lack of a better word.

The "How" of turning up the rheostat

Psychologists say that *thinking* about something is quite different from *believing* it, and that a thought or idea can become
a belief and positioned in consciousness as a reality only if it
remains uncontradicted. (Think how many times each day you
deny your good by contradicting what you want to believe.)

William James, founder of one of the first psychological labo-
ratories in this country, said that a belief can be embodied in
consciousness through "the path of emotions" and "the path of
will." Regarding the emotions, he wrote that the idea or concept
must first appear "both interesting and important." The idea,
therefore, must be one that excites and stimulates our interest.
The interest will then stimulate the emotions — particularly feelings of love, and when the feeling reaches the stage of "passion"
it is recorded as a belief in the mind.

Concerning "the path of will"—he wrote: "Gradually our will can lead us to the same results by a very simple method. We need only act as if the thing in question was real, and keep acting as if it were real, and it will infallibly end by growing into such a connection with our life that it will become real. It will become so knit with habit and emotion that our interest in it will be those which characterize belief."[3]

To strengthen our beliefs, let's combine the two paths in a seven-step program.

Step No. 1: The first thing we must do is clear out the negative energy of resentment in our consciousness. I have found that this particular frequency of energy is a most destructive force in not only tearing down positive beliefs, but in also creating the greatest possible variety of fears. Now in case you do not know what "resentment" means, it is defined in the dictionary as "a feeling of indignant displeasure at something regarded as a wrong, insult or injury." How do we eliminate resentment? Go to your dictionary again and look up "forgive"—which is defined as "to cease to feel resentment against—to give up resentment."

The beautiful thing about forgiving is that your deeper-than-conscious mind will act to release you from the attachment of resentment even if you only *want* to forgive and cannot at the time evoke the feeling of loving forgiveness in your heart. In other words, the *will to forgive* is sufficient to begin the cleansing action. Knowing that any kind of resentment (unforgiveness) toward anyone or anything is blocking your good, you can now *want* to forgive through your power of will.

Open your spiritual journal to the next blank page, date it, and start listing everything and anyone you can possibly think of that/who has ever caused you "indignant displeasure." Go back as far as you can remember and write down every hurt, every insult, every mental-emotional-physical injury received from someone. Think of the people, places, situations and conditions that you have disliked and write them down. Think of every experience that has polluted your consciousness with negative energy and add them to your list.

And if you do not have the following on your list, please add them: Your parents, your children, everyone who has ever been on this planet and who is here now, your world, God, and yourself. Totally forgive all!

When your inventory is complete, start right at the top and slowly move down the list, bringing each image into your mind and saying:

I forgive you completely. I hold no unforgiveness back. My forgiveness for you is total. I am free and you are free!

Once you have completed this cleansing action, make a note in your journal that beginning that very night you will continue your forgiveness work by forgiving everyone whom you feel has not been released from your emotional attachment. Make it a habit to spend a few minutes every single evening at bedtime to forgive those who still cause a dip in your consciousness, plus anyone from that particular day who has caused you "indignant displeasure." Do not go to sleep with any unforgiveness in your heart!

Step No. 2: Write the following statement in your journal:

I want to believe with all my heart that the One Presence and Power of the Universe is in total control of my life. I want to believe in God as the One Source of all my good.

Speak these words aloud, then again silently. Remember that energy follows thought, so as you ponder these words with great feeling, know that the pure energy of this desire is penetrating into your consciousness to do its creative work. It is important that you repeat this statement as often as possible during the first day of the new program — preferably every hour. After the first day it will not be necessary to repeat this step.

Step No. 3: Totally explore your consciousness and write in your journal everything you think you believe about God. The step is simply a benchmark to show you later how far you've come, and does not have to be repeated unless you so desire.

Step No. 4: Answer this question in your journal: "What is *my* relationship to God at the present time?" Let your thoughts flow. This step will not have to be repeated.

Step No. 5: Answer this question according to your present understanding: "How would God describe His relationship with me?" This step will not have to be repeated.

Step No. 6: Open your heart and mind and answer this question fully: "What kind of relationship with God do I choose?" It will not be necessary to repeat this step either.

Step No. 7: We are now ready to use a form of the Manifestation Process—and it is suggested that you follow this treatment sequence for a minimum of seven days.

Go to a quiet place, sit up straight and take several deep breaths to clear your mind and settle your emotions.

Now imagine that someone has walked up behind you and is standing there looking at you. You feel the stare and you are so aware of this presence that the entire vibration of your feeling nature is beginning to change. Imagine now that this presence is invisible, a Being of Light and an all-knowing Mind, and that the Presence is slowly moving into you, penetrating your body, your mind, your emotional nature, your entire consciousness with Itself. Feel the surge of power as this Being of Light and Love moves in to occupy the same space that you do. Sense the intense Knowingness of Its Mind as It thinks within your consciousness. See the Light saturating your entire being.

Understand that through this exercise you have become aware of your God-Self, the Spirit of God within you.

Next, see a white screen in your mind and on this screen see the words I CHOOSE with lines following as if on a ruled tablet. Now in your own handwriting fill in the blank spaces with these words:

(I CHOOSE)...*to realize a loving relationship with my God-Self.*

Focus on each word with great clarity and then say to yourself silently:

I accept the fulfillment of this desire now. With all my mind, all my heart, all my soul, I accept this fulfillment now. And because I have accepted the Idea of all that this relationship means, I now have it. I now have the conscious link in my oneness with my God-Self, and I love the feeling of HAVING in my heart.

Now in the chamber of your imagination, see yourself totally enjoying your relationship with the inner Christ Presence, the Reality of you. See yourself awakening in the morning and joyfully greeting the Presence with a heart-felt "Good Morning!" See and hear yourself telling that Being of Light within that you love It with all your mind, heart, soul and strength. See yourself dressing and expressing gratitude for your clothes, and for the opportunity to be of special service to all God's expressions throughout the day. See yourself taking time for meditation and feeling the beautiful loving contact with Spirit. Listen and "hear" — in your imagination — your glorious Higher Self speak to you..."I will never leave you nor forsake you. I am with you always, for you are my expression, the light of my Light."

Let the words continue in your inner ear — words of Light and Love and Peace and Wholeness and Abundance and Harmony and Protection. See yourself going about your day *feeling* the Presence within, talking to the Presence, listening to the Presence, walking with the Presence, laughing with the Presence, thanking the Presence, loving the Presence. See yourself literally having a love affair with the Christ within. Sense the experience with your mind. Feel the experience with your heart. See the experience clearly with your inner eye.

After several minutes of visualizing the beautiful oneness of this new relationship, say to yourself with great feeling:

Oh how I love what I see. I love these images of my relationship with my God-Self, the Reality of me. I love the Oneness. I love the Wholeness. And I feel the love throughout my being!

Rest in the silence for a few minutes, then speak the Word, aloud if possible:

The one all-Intelligent Power of the Universe is around and in and through me at this very moment. This Infinite Love is right now healing my body, prospering my affairs, harmonizing my relationships, giving me every good gift, adjusting all conditions, straightening out every crooked place, perfecting all that concerns me, and totally protecting me from all harm and from every negative influence.

Oh my God. . .this is really happening to me right now! And it's happening because You love me! The Power of the Universe is in love with me! And oh how I love you! The Bond of Love is complete and the sense of separation is gone. I believe this totally. I believe this completely. All darkness is gone. There is now only the Light of absolute belief. And through this perfect belief in God, every cell of my body has been renewed, the creative substance has manifested as my abundant supply, and unconditional Love has permeated my world. Oh Christ, it has happened! I feel it! I know it! The Universe is for me! God loves me! I don't have to fight anymore. There is nothing to fear anymore. It is done. . .and it is so!

Rest for a period in the silence.

Now with great love and thankfulness in your heart, turn within and say:

I now totally surrender my mortal mind, ego and personality to the Spirit within, knowing that the Activity of God now taking place within me and through me is the only Power at work in my life and affairs. With complete gratitude I surrender to the Love of my heart and soul.

Now you are ready to move into action—which is absolutely necessary to maintain the belief system at the highest level until it "locks in" as a complete realization. And this is where "the path of will" comes into play. Recall the role that you assumed in your creative visualization where you devoted the day to enjoying your relationship with the inner Christ Presence. This is what you must do now in actual practice. And you must play the role with all the emotion, excitement, fullness of heart, passion, fervor, warmth and love that you can feel—not leaving out one single activity of your daily life where Spirit is not participating.

Talk with Spirit. Laugh with Spirit. Play with Spirit. Love with Spirit. And you know what? It will not be long before this ideal relationship becomes Real for you, and when it does, your life will change so dramatically that you will scarcely remember the old you and all those haunting fears. You will be *fear-less*!

6

Uniting Mind and Heart

Two of the most risky states of consciousness prevalent today are represented by (1) those with a total abandonment to living third-dimensionally, and (2) the absolutists who talk endlessly about the perfection of God and man, but refuse to be a co-creator in bringing that perfection into visibility and experience.

Both of these states of mind are really based on spiritual inertia—and I used the word "risky" in describing them because when you try to lose yourself in either the whirling fog of the physical plane—or in fourth dimensional passivity—it can certainly be hazardous to your spiritual health.

Yes, there is a fine line, a straight and narrow path that we must walk, and it can best be described as a state of mind where the individual lives in the fourth dimension (spiritual consciousness) and expresses in the third dimension (physical world) as a co-creator with God. How do we do this? One way is by aligning the powers of Will and Love in a vertical rod, or beam of Light, and expressing them simultaneously as courage, strength of purpose, resolution, and determination to be active as a spiritual being—and as total unconditional love toward everyone and everything. To help you establish that bridge between mind and heart, let's look at a few facts:

1. You are here to awaken to your own divinity.

2. You are here to help others awaken to their divinity.

3. You are here to participate in the salvation of the world.

4. You cannot awaken to your own divinity until you have a sense of responsibility to others and to the world.

5. You cannot feel a responsibility to others and to the world until you begin to take control of the lower self.

6. You cannot correct the lower self until you activate the power of will and begin to use this force to discipline the personality.

7. Through your will you develop a sense of firmness, stability, dedication and purpose in your life...a one-pointed focus on realizing the Truth of your being and the healing of humankind on a global scale.

8. The focus of will alone may be expressed as the cold determination to move through any obstacle at any cost.

9. When blended with the love energy, the power of will broadens its perspective and accepts its responsibility as a member of the planetary family. Its actions are then based on the divine idea of Goodwill.

10. When love is centered exclusively in the feeling nature and not balanced by mind (will), the individual may become over-sensitive to the illusions of this world and feel deep-seated emotional hurts over apparent injustices. This is conditional love based on attachments, rather than unconditional love which is completely detached from illusion.

11. When combined with the force of will, the unconditional love energy becomes the Great Harmonizer in your life and affairs, the supplier for the aims of will, and the provider for every need.

12. Through unconditional love (no strings attached), you transmute the negative energy of the lower self and you begin to feel a sense of responsibility to others and to the planet.

13. Once you begin to look beyond the lower self, you begin to awaken to your own divinity.

14. In the awakening process, your life's mission and purpose will be revealed with greater clarity.

15. Once you have your "piece of the puzzle" you will be drawn to the place, people and opportunities where the Divine

Plan for your life can be implemented in all its fullness.

A closer look at the Will faculty

Will is the directive power of consciousness and is closely linked with choice, decision and decree. When the will is focused on spiritual ideals, you are moving toward the Christ Connection. And as you are willing to "be about the Father's business" — you are reconnecting the purpose of the lower nature with the Will of the Higher Self, and this true I AM can then express the fullness of Its potentiality in and through your consciousness.

Watch what happens in your energy field when you speak these declarations with power:

I am determined to be all that I was created to be!

I choose to express the fullness of my Christhood!

I now make a conscious decision to step out into mastery in this lifetime!

I decree a full awakening to the Christ within!

I now link my will with the Will of my Higher Self and move forward to fulfill my mission and purpose in this incarnation!

I will achieve my destiny!

I will fulfill my mission!

Did you sense the power, the determination, the feeling of commitment? This is the consciousness of the Spiritual Warrior where nothing is impossible! The will faculty, which is located in your energy field near the front center of the brain, is now glowing with radiant light, and like steam in a boiler, its force will propel you toward your destination — literally rolling over every seeming obstacle. But without the balancing effect of love, will can be a power out of control, with the "end justifying the means" becoming the primary motivation.

Think of it this way: In the Mind of God, "will" means the Cosmic Urge to express, and that expression is always with and in love, meaning the highest Good-for-all. Your will is your urge to express the fullness of your potentiality, but the radiating force must be controlled by unconditional love. Mind and emotions, head and heart, must be united in and for **Goodwill**.

Hooking up with the energy of Love

When will is brought into alignment with love, your vision becomes broader and your consciousness is lifted into a higher vibration. You continue to move toward your objective, but that objective now includes freedom, joy, peace, abundance, wholeness and happiness, not only for yourself, but for all humanity. The drive of will combined with the energy of love from the heart center makes you a Lightbearer—a blessing to everyone within the range of your consciousness. Also, the will-to-Good (the unity of will and love), will eliminate spiritual inertia, will lift your gaze above the purely physical world, and will transform absolute passivity into spiritual action.

Try this exercise with me. First, see with your inner eye a vertical rod (beam) of Light connecting the love faculty in your heart to the power of will in the high center of your forehead. Let your awareness and feelings run up and down the beam. As you inhale, move with the Light from the heart up to the head; as you exhale, move down the beam of Light from the head to the heart. Breathe deeply as you practice the connecting of these two powers, devoting two or three minutes to the exercise.

Next, concentrate on your heart center and say with deep feeling:

I love the Self I was created to be.

(pause and take a deep breath after each statement)

Now place your attention on the high center of your forehead and say with great strength of will and purpose of mind:

I am determined to realize the Self that I was created to be!

Down to the heart with feeling:

I love my Self.

Up to the head with firmness and power:

I now make the conscious decision to be my Self!

Down to the heart:

I love every Soul on this planet and beyond as my Self.

Up to the head:

I choose wholeness and harmony for everyone without exception!

Down to the heart:

I love this world!
Up to the head:
I am determined to do my part as a healing channel!
Down to the heart:
I love the activity of Spirit in my life and in the lives of all others.
Up to the head:
I am the activity of Spirit as a distributor of God Power!
Down to the heart:
I love my mission in life!
Up to the head:
I now go forth with great enthusiasm to accomplish that which Spirit has for me to do!

The uniting of these two powers will balance your energies, start your "engine" and press the accelerator to give you the go-power to move toward your destination with loving determination. By connecting the powers of love and will and expressing them in your daily life, you will receive all the inspiration, guidance and enthusiasm you need to chart your course, pull up the anchor, and move out to find your piece of the puzzle. And as you do, you'll notice those "challenges" falling away and vanishing from your life because you will be moving out of the low vibration of the lower self where problems find entrance into your life and affairs.

Use your will to build a fire under you and to get your momentum going—and let love point the way and be the guiding light to the mountaintop!

7

What Are You Saying and Seeing?

Two of the most effective tools that we can use in our work of practical spirituality are the spoken word and creative visualization. When used properly, in a feeling of love and with an awareness of the Spirit within, beautiful adjustments can be made in your life and affairs. But again, these are *tools* — as are the techniques of written affirmations, cord-cutting, list-making, letters to angels, treasure mapping, wheels of fortune, and others. The key is to use whatever tool, treatment or technique that is most effective for you to create new conditions as you move up the ladder in consciousness. Just keep in mind that your ultimate goal is to realize the Presence of God within you and let that Realization (the Christ Consciousness) interpret Itself as every needed thing in your life. This is living by Grace. However, while you are moving toward this Destination, develop and use your powers as a learning and growing child of God.

The Spoken Word of Power

The Power of Authority, or the Power of the Word, is an energy drawn in through the vortex lying in the etheric anatomy of the throat. Everytime you speak, you set the Power in motion...you release a surge of creative energy vibrating to the idea behind the particular word that was spoken. And the vibration established in substance will produce an effect corresponding to the idea verbalized. As Job put it, "Thou shalt also decree a thing, and it shall be established unto thee."

The spoken word is an awesome power, and we must learn to use it correctly. Ernest Holmes (in *Science of Mind*[1]) wrote, "The word gives form to the unformed. The greater the consciousness behind the word, the more power it will have." And in *Dynamics for Living*,[2] Charles Fillmore said, "If man conformed to the divine law, his word would make things instantly." The Bible also gives us a few admonitions regarding the spoken word—for example, "By your words you will be justified, and by your words you will be condemned." (Matthew 12:37) and... "Death and life are in the power of the tongue." (Proverbs 18:21)

Let's take a close look at four specific points regarding the spoken word:

1. **The consciousness behind the word is the power.** Consciousness means the total collection of your thoughts, feelings and beliefs molded into a structure of awareness, understanding and knowledge of the visible and invisible worlds. You verbalize your consciousness when you speak. Consciousness is the cause, and the word propels the energy according to the vibration of consciousness, and the resulting manifestation is the effect. Therefore, when you speak the word you are projecting *your* consciousness into the phenomenal world to create or change forms and conditions, and the effect is always in accordance with the cause.

2. **Positive words spoken from a sense of deep-seated fear or negative emotions may breed even more fearful and negative conditions.** You can't fake it. Saying "I am rich" from a poverty consciousness will not make you wealthy. It may even accent the poverty vibration if the mind grasps the idea of futility while the word is being spoken. And to affirm that you are experiencing a loving relationship when you are desperately lonely can trigger an emotional response underlining the idea of loneliness, which will then be aggravated by your spoken word.

Many years ago, when I first discovered that the words we

speak have power, I used this tool with great effectiveness. Later, when things were a little dark on the horizon, I began to decree that my business was wonderfully successful, that money rolled in in avalanches of abundance, and that new clients appeared daily enabling us to expand the staff and facilities. Well, just the opposite happened — and the reason was because the idea behind the words was contrary to the decree. The parent idea was a belief that I had a sick business, that the bank account was drying up, and that we were losing clients rather than adding new ones. So my spoken word was contrary to what I really believed, and my consciousness was outpictured with even greater velocity through fearful words dressed up to look like positive affirmations.

I realized this when I began to listen to my idle words — words spoken about the business when I wasn't trying to watch my thoughts or words. And I was truly shocked by what was coming out of my mouth, which was the **true** reflection of my consciousness. In essence, my casual, unthinking and offhand remarks were coming from the heart (how I really felt), and we recall from Proverbs 4:23 — "Keep your heart with all vigilance; from it flows the springs of life." And, according to Jesus, ". . . men will render account for every careless word they utter." (Matthew 12:36) Yes, we are accountable for words from the heart that are placed in the cause and effect process.

3. **Words spoken from a negative consciousness will create conditions corresponding to that state of mind.** Words are the verbal expressions of ideas. Ideas verbalized from a negative consciousness have the power to create negative conditions. If you feel that you will never recover from that physical ailment and that you will "just have to live with it" — and you speak the words accordingly — the universe will honor your decree. Remember, every word is a prayer, and when we pray, believing, we always get what we pray for. So even if you "believe" that you don't have enough money to meet your needs, for heaven's sake don't verbalize it! When you are in a lower vibration (negative) consciousness, there are two things to do: First, keep your lips sealed and your tongue still, oth-

erwise that idle chatter will be propelling negative energy into the world of form to emphasize and accentuate that which you do not want.

There is an old Chinese proverb that says: "We have two ears and two eyes, but one tongue, in order that we may see and hear twice as much as we speak."

After you've zipped your mouth, the next thing to do is to move out of that negative consciousness through meditation and spiritual treatment—even if you have to spend forty days in the desert. If your suit or dress catches fire, you don't stand around watching the flames...you immediately take action to put the fire out. Same thing with consciousness. If you start to burn with negative energy, don't wait to do something about it later. Take immediate action to reconnect with the Spirit within you!

4. **Words spoken from a spiritual consciousness have power to mold substance and create positive experiences.** "Spiritual consciousness" means being in tune with Spirit—the state of mind and heart that you feel when you have gone within and have touched the Light. When you are in this higher consciousness and speak the word with a clearly-defined purpose, you are establishing a particular vibration in substance. And as this vibration is "stepped down" it becomes a force field that manifests in visible forms and conditions according to the Idea behind the spoken word.

Remember that everything in the manifest world is an expression of an invisible Idea, and the use of the spoken word is but one way to work with the law of cause and effect to bring the Idea into visibility.

Techniques in using the spoken word

In writing your decrees or spoken treatments, it is important that you begin by identifying the Source of all Power, and then identify yourself with that Power. You should know exactly what it is that you are speaking the word for—making sure that it is not a selfish decree, that you are affirming for yourself what you truly desire for everyone else. Be certain that you are not trying to infringe on anyone's free will. Decree that the fulfillment you seek will come forth according to the Will and Way of Spirit, and conclude with "It is done!"

Now let's use Words of Power incorporating the above ingredients. We will speak the word for prosperity, but you can change the words to express any type of fulfillment you are seeking.

Begin by relaxing, taking several deep breaths, and focusing your attention on the Spirit within you. Contemplate the absolute Faith, Strength, Wisdom, Love and Will of your Christ Self, drawing those Divine Energies into your consciousness and identifying with them. Then speak these words aloud with great feeling:

The Mind and Energy of Infinite Abundance is the one Presence and Power of the universe.

This Mind, Energy, Presence and Power is individualized as me now.

I, (your name), am the perfect expression of infinite abundance and boundless prosperity.

That which I desire, I AM. All that I could ever seek, I have. I am abundance, therefore, I have abundance.

That which I decree for myself, I decree for all according to each Soul's choice and acceptance.

I now release this Word of Power to the Will and Way of Spirit, knowing that the action of abundance is now taking place in my life.

It is done!

Now get up and go about your business, putting all thought of the spoken word out of your mind. Continue daily speaking words of Power until you achieve the fulfillment you are seeking.

Creative Visualization

A few years ago I had a bi-location experience where I seemed to be in two places at the same time. . . in my bedroom with Jan and in a beautiful white temple where I was talking to the old man who appears frequently in my dreams. But this was not a dream! It was very real as I could feel, see, hear and smell with my senses in both locations at the same time.

As I sat across from the man in the temple, I began to ask questions, and he would answer each question with a question. Staring at me with arms crossed over his heart, he constantly asked: "What do you see?" That's all he ever said in nearly an hour. After a while I could feel myself getting a bit frustrated with the repetition, and it was probably this dissatisfaction with the conversation that suddenly pulled the traveling part of me back into oneness with the other "me" there at home with Jan.

I thought about the experience for the rest of the night, and meditated on it the following day. Several different interpretations came through. I saw the planet as desperately needing help, and I was being stimulated to think about the service that I could provide. "Seeing" also means understanding, so I felt that the Understanding faculty in my energy field needed to be brought up to a higher vibratory level. Also, the True Self sees only perfection and wholeness. . . so I was being told to see as Spirit sees — the Reality behind the illusion. And later, Jan showed me a quote from *The Superbeings*. It was on Page 2 where I referred to Dr. Donald Hatch Andrews, Professor Emeritus of Chemistry at Johns Hopkins University. He said: "It is not seeing with the eye but seeing with the mind that gives us a basis for belief, and in this way science and religion are one. We are now entering an age when we will hold the power of life in our hands, and if it is to be used properly it must be in a world dominated by love. What we must have in this world today is a chain reaction of the human spirit. It we can feel this vision and if we can act on it, if we can transmit this vision to others and persuade everyone that living in terms of the spirit is the only answer, then we can change the face of the world."

What really stood out for both of us were these words: *"It is seeing with the mind"* — and — *"If we can feel this vision."* In other words, we must *see* and *feel* the vision by uniting the mind and the heart. We must see with the inner vision and not just with the eyes, and we must feel what we see in our hearts. Perhaps each interpretation of the old man's question was correct, but this last one seemed to bring them all together in a very practical answer.

What we're really talking about here is *creative* visualization. And we see that it has an added dimension, a dual purpose: (1) the visioning process keeps the will faculty highly energized and maintains the love vibration at a finer pitch, and (2) visualization is a tool that we can use in co-creating with Spirit. Let's discuss both points.

Staying on the beam with creative visualization. I have found in my experience that whenever my motivation and enthusiasm start to lag, it simply means that the directive power of my consciousness (will) has taken a downward turn. I can be wonderfully loving during these blahs, but I don't have the inspiration to soar — to fly high — in accomplishing my reason for being. That's when it is time to call on the power of imagination to "feed" my mind with pictures for the visioning process. As I call forth the scenario of my Life Program and lovingly see myself doing, being, having according to Spirit's Script, my entire energy field begins to perk and a whole new vibration of zest and vitality takes over.

To be filled with a "directive power" in consciousness, you need a sense of direction for your power of will. This is why I frequently urge people to research their Divine Plan and develop their Life Program as discussed in Chapter Three of *The Planetary Commission* — "The Divine Plan." Look at it this way: Your Life Program points you in the direction of your highest vision. The power of will is then activated to diligently follow that course of action. Through unconditional love you move beyond self and become more universal in consciousness in accomplishing your purpose. And if the directive power starts to veer off course, you use the power of imagination to "lock in" again to the High Vision and get back on track.

Yes, the answer to "what do you see?" can cause a powerful and positive reaction in your energy field. Visualization can be the cosmic fuel to help you reach the stars.

Using visualization to co-create with Spirit. It is interesting that one of the initial teachings in the mystery schools of the ancient past was the art of visualization. And one reason that it was part of the introduction to the mysteries was based on the knowledge that energy follows thought — and when there is clarity of vision, the creative energy manifests the vision in the physical world. As Barbara Marx Hubbard has said, "As we see ourselves, so we tend to become." That is the law!

The key to visualization is to lovingly and clearly concentrate with the full power of mind on the experiences you wish to objectify. There must be continuity in your images and not a scattered series of pictures with no relation to one another. You should also begin by focusing on your primary objective, and then move on to the next one.

To commence the process you take the same steps as you would in going into meditation. Sit quietly and take several deep breaths to relax the mind and body...then begin to contemplate the presence within, the Spirit of your Self, and feel the love vibration in your heart. Now silently command that your Imagination faculty awaken and work in accordance with the Vision of Spirit. At this point, see in your mind's eye a blank white screen and let your imagination project the images of your fulfilled desires on the screen. Control the pictures so that you see, feel, hear and smell only the totally positive experience that you desire, and concentrate on the images until every detail is etched in your consciousness.

Once this is done, close the curtain on the screen in your mind and forget about the visualization process until you can repeat the same *controlled* procedure in your next meditative treatment. The reason for this is to keep you from diluting or scattering the energy building up around the thought-form, the same energy that will carry the image into visibility.

Here's another tip to make your imaging more effective: Regardless of what you are "seeing" to manifest as a visible experience, find the most pleasurable and joyous point in the scenario for the period of concentration. You will have to find that point for yourself, but whether you are visualizing lavish abundance, a soul mate relationship, a perfect body, true place success, the total awakening to your spiritual Identity, or the healing and harmonizing of the planet, there is a "scene" that portrays fulfillment, wholeness and completion more than any other—and it is upon that scene that you should concentrate your energy.

Also remember that the *clearer* the picture you see...the *longer* you can hold it in mind before it "breaks up"...and the *deeper* you can feel the vision...the *faster* the materialization.

8

Guides and Guidance

The subject of guides and the sources of guidance has fascinated me for years. We have all had those flashes of inspiration, intuition and illumination, but how many of us have paused for a moment to consider the source of the motivation and understanding, and then express our gratitude for the guidance?

When I first began to study New Thought concepts and the Wisdom Teachings, I attributed special guidance to my subconscious. Through "programming" of this faithful servant to guide and inspire me, specific impressions and impulses were brought into my conscious mind. But the subjective patterns for guidance were based on relative conditions and precedents because I was programming out of a relative consciousness. So the guidance was either a bit distorted, or simply reflected the desires that had already been registered subjectively.

Later, as my consciousness expanded and I began to recognize a deeper level of Mind, I felt that my Higher Self was the guiding, guarding, harmonizing influence in my life. But I also became aware of something else. The guidance from the Superconsciousness came forth on a specific wavelength or vibration, which I could recognize—but at other times I would receive an impression or message which seemed to come in on another channel with a different vibration.

At first I attributed these changes in vibratory communications to shifts in my own consciousness, but I still considered the source to be the Christ Mind or Superconsciousness within. Then I began to realize that the communications from this Higher Self would only come through when I was in tune with that Self—when there was a similar vibration in consciousness. Accordingly, I considered the idea that the different channel of communications, which seemed to be activated when I was not in that Christ Vibration, represented another "sender." This was when I began to think about guardian angels, guides, and Souls beyond the veil offering a helping hand.

Think about it. During or following meditation, you have felt an inner knowing regarding a decision to make, or you have received new understanding on the Nature of God and your Self as an Expression of the Infinite. This happened when you were in the Upper Room of consciousness and were partaking of the Christ Energy. But also remember those other times when you were solidly entrenched in sense consciousness and a new idea or inspiration hit you from out of the blue. Didn't these communications seem to come from different points in your energy field and with different vibratory rates?

The one Guide

One day, while meditating on these different "channels of communications"—the Voice within said, "There is only one Mind, one Voice, one Guide." I knew this was the truth, but I also intuitively felt by this time that there were invisible Teachers or Guides active in all of our lives. So in my meditations I began seeking the answer to how the multiple channels were all really one Voice, and I received an understanding that I would like to share with you. To do so, I'm going to take a roundabout way to explain it, so please bear with me.

First, let's refer to Page 98 in *The Planetary Commission*: "Can you understand now that the only difference between the Universal Spirit of God and the Individualized Spirit of God *you are* is but a change in vibration? It is a stepping down in frequency to where the Universe says 'I AM.' This I AM is God...this I AM is You...Universal *and* Individual Consciousness...God knowing Itself as God, God knowing Itself as You, and You knowing Yourself as God. The Ancients taught that this Reality of You forever remains in the Absolute, and in order to express the cosmic urge of Its infinite Will, there must be a channel or vehicle for expression. Therefore, your Spirit conceived within Its Mind the Idea of Itself in expression as a living Soul. This has been called 'the second creation' where you became a self-conscious entity, created in the Image and Likeness of your Self, the Spirit of God. However, rather than separating Itself, which It could not do, your God-Self followed the original creative Process and changed the vibratory rate within the center of Its Individualized Energy Field. In this 'pressed out' state of consciousness, you knew yourself to be a spiritual being, a Son of God, forever living within the Mind of Spirit and filled with the pure awareness of your God-Self."

And from Page 74 in the same book: "When you came to dwell in the material plane and took on a physical body, a part of your Soul consciousness was lowered in vibration for the purpose of grounding and functioning on the third-dimensional plane...(and) in time, the lower vibration of Soul in the dense physical body became conscious of only the third-dimensional world. From the realm of Grace you descended into the province of karma and came under the law of cause and effect. Now there was a sense of separation as the Higher Soul remained one with Spirit as the Christ Consciousness, while the lower soul dropped further into the darkness of the mortal ego."

Now...at the time of the "sense of separation" something very dramatic and significant happened. Because the Higher Soul or Superconsciousness had no awareness of the separation (was not aware of the personality or newly-formed ego), an Aspect of Spirit known as Active Intelligence or Universal Inspiration was "sent forth" to become the dominant Energy in the realm of the Superconsciousness. Its purpose: to radiate Light and illumine the lower mental-emotional faculties. With this "Shining" upon and within the lower self, each individual had a sure Guide back to the Father's House and a Comforter to share the journey — because this "Holy Spirit" Aspect of God sees both above and below... the Reality of God and the illusions of man.

This means that the pure I AM Spirit, the Whole Christ Spirit embodying the fullness of the Godhead, reflected Itself in your Soul at the time of the descent into the illusion of the separation, giving it another dimension of Consciousness. The Circle of Vision was now complete, and the activity of Spirit working in and *as* the Soul or Superconsciousness could then reflect Itself in the lower self to bring you back into conscious at-one-ment with your Higher Self.

The call to remembrance

To help you grasp the significance of this, I'll relate a personal experience. For quite some time, I had felt and seen (inner vision) a Presence hovering in my consciousness. It was as though my consciousness was a dimly-lit room and standing in the doorway was a Presence of Light, and I could strongly sense Its intense Knowingness, Love and Power. From the moment of that first dawning, I could "connect" with that Presence whenever I brought my mind into a conscious awareness of It. To me, this was my Higher Soul, my Christ Consciousness, and I referred to this Presence in a variety of terms: Soul, Lord, Superconsciousness, Higher Self, Christ Mind, Spirit, and anything else that felt comfortable at the time. Then one day I asked, "Who are you?" And the answer was: "I AM. I AM all that you are... I AM the Spirit of God... I AM the call to remembrance." I knew at that moment that my spiritual essence was so much more than I had every conceived. I was more than mind, emotions and body... I was more than a soul simply being "aware" of a Presence within my consciousness... I was THAT PRESENCE! I AM IT! And so are you!

There is no duality. There is not God *and* you...there is only God *as* you. And this God-You will lead you back into the realization of your true Identity!

What does this have to do with guides? Well, the point is, there is only *one* Guide because each Individual *is* the same Spirit. The Active Intelligence and Knowingness of Spirit is the essence and energy of every Consciousness on this side of the veil or the other. There is but one Guide, and that is the very Vision, Wisdom, Energy and Power of the Universal Christ pressing out (expressing) *as* the Spirit of all. So whether the Voice is speaking from your Christ Self or through a Guide, it is still the same Voice reaching you at different vibratory levels. The Spirit in me and the Spirit in my guides is the same Spirit! The Spirit in you and the Spirit in your guides is the same Spirit! There is but one Guide, one Voice, yet It uses different channels to reach you depending on the vibration of your consciousness. And over the years I've also met many men and women in physical form who just happened to say something to me that opened my mind and heart to a new understanding. Where was this new Light coming from? From the one Spirit, the one Voice, speaking to me from the particular man or woman. Each channel for Spirit has a distinct role to play in your spiritual evolution.

Your Spirit is constantly flooding the chambers of the lower mental and emotional faculties to awaken you to the glory that is yours as a Son of God and lead you back to the Father's House. In the Awakening Process, the mysteries of the Kingdom are revealed and the Path of Discipleship is unfolded. But if your vibration is too low or scattered to receive the Light, the Divine Inspiration will be of little benefit. This is where your guides come in. Now, as we said, the Spirit in you and the Spirit in your guides is the same Spirit, and although each guide is "interpreting" Spirit according to his/her level of consciousness, his or her primary purpose is to help you during the low vibration states to bring your lower nature under the control of your Soul. (The only true Teacher is within you.) This is done primarily through energy impulses stepped down to the vibration where you are at the time. As the vibration increases through these impulses, your Soul Light can begin the process of transmuting or purifying the lower nature, and the Journey Home progresses.

Once you are on the Path, the role of your guides is to inspire you to action in the service of others, and ultimately to world service. Their function is also to protect you when necessary through streams of force (energy) to alert you to an unforeseen danger, and to guide you in the implementation of your life plan. But again, there is but one Guide, one Voice, using different channels to reach you depending on the vibration of your consciousness. This includes channeling. If you hear an entity speaking through a physical apparatus, and you intuitively feel that the message is "Right" for you, then understand that you are listening to the Voice within your very Self. But be very discerning!

Speaking of channeled information, permit me to share with you part of a conversation that Jan and I had with an entity called "John" speaking through a trance-medium in Huntington, New York. This was in October 1984, and I had asked about guides. Here are excerpts from the answer:

"Each physical will have at least three guides who will be with them for the course of their physical life. In addition to those three guides, there will be others who will come and go according to the needs of the individual. These guides may in many ways be compared to your physical family — your physical circle of friends. Those guides who will be with you during the course of an entire lifetime will be individuals with whom you have shared experiences usually in other physical lives. They will be ones who share love for you, with you, who have an interest in your growth. Many times there will exist between an individual and their guides a karmic relationship as well. Those guides who will be with you for a shorter period of your time are very much like your friends. Guides will work with an individual...they will provide what they can provide for that individual, and then they will move on and allow another guide to come along. Consider your guides simply as non-physical friends."

Personal comments about guide and guidance

1. You are never alone. You have a constant Guide, Companion and Comforter with you at all times Who knows exactly where you are in consciousness, the state of your affairs and how to straighten out every crooked place in your life. But more than just knowing, It is *doing*! It is doing everything for you now! Seek first the relationship with your Spirit and It will experience Itself as every needed thing in your Life.

2. The more time you spend in loving, contemplative meditation — dwelling on the Spirit of You — the more active and louder the "still, small voice" will be.

3. When you ask Spirit for guidance, you will *always* receive an answer — directly from within or from your guides. Stay open and listen!

4. Know that even when you have lost conscious contact with Spirit within through "busy-ness" in the outer world, that same Spirit is working through your guides on different vibratory levels. Follow your intuition!

5. Do not pray to your guides. Simply acknowledge their presence and express gratitude for their assistance.

6. Your true helpers will only radiate love, joy and serenity — and will never guide you to do something contrary to the Christ Standard.

7. Be careful that reliance on guidance does not put you into a permanent state of inactivity. I've seen people wait for answers and directions so long that they were covered in cobwebs. Take the action you feel is right for the good-of-all and rely on Spirit to make any necessary adjustments along the way.

8. Never forget that you have free will! You are not a robot waiting for someone to program you. You are the master of your own destiny — and not the servant of some "master" whose role is to tell you what to do.

9. Use great spiritual discernment if someone tells you that he/she is in direct communications with a master, and that he/she has a "special message" just for you.

10. Neither every impulse you feel, nor every voice you hear is Spirit. A state of mind that is too passive and with a low spiritual vibration may interpret subconscious desires as the

guidance of God, or may contact a discarnate with a negative consciousness and consider the impressions as the Voice of Spirit. Keep yourself surrounded with the White Light and know that true Guidance is always based on the highest good of all!

11. Repeat this thought to yourself frequently: "The Spirit of (your name) speaks to me through every channel, visible and invisible. There is but one Voice, and I am only receptive to it."

12. When you seek the advice and counsel of others, always hold in mind that Spirit is speaking to you through them.

13. When you see or consciously think of another person, always recognize/acknowledge the Spirit within him/her. Practice this and witness the beneficial effect upon everyone including yourself.

14. The more you are consciously aware of the Spirit in yourself and others, the stronger your guidance for Right Action will be.

15. The greater your realization of Spirit, the less guidance you will seek, for Spirit will be fulfilling Itself through you, as you, without you "taking thought."

9

Twelve Doors to Mastery

Here is a checklist to determine where you are in the awakening process.

1. Have you experienced the Birth of Truth in your consciousness? Can you truly say that Christ lives within you, and that you can feel this Truth of your Being growing stronger day by day as the Light expands in your heart and mind?

2. Once you have experienced the New Birth, did you hide the Christ Truth in consciousness to protect it from the destructive power of your ego and the ego of others?

3. Are you growing in your understanding of the Law of Cause and Effect so that you are now working with the Presence as a co-creator?

4. Have you purified your emotional nature with a thorough cleansing, and are you continuing to maintain your energy field in that clear and clean condition?

5. Have you developed the spiritual strength and understanding to overcome the temptations of the ego?

6. Have you consented to the soul's call to perform "miracles" through the transmutation of negative energy?

7. Have you awakened your inner powers so that they may unite in perfect harmony in your consciousness?

8. Have you moved beyond concern for yourself to a focus on world service and what you can do for others?

9. Have the personality and individuality been unified to where your lower and higher natures are perfectly integrated?

10. Has the personality been crossed out and the human consciousness replaced with the Divine Consciousness?

11. Have you fully realized your Divinity and are you now living exclusively in the Christ Consciousness as the Risen Christ?

12. Have you ascended into total Mastery through a complete merging with the Will of God?

These questions refer to the Twelve Doors to Mastery, sometimes called initiations, or expansions in consciousness, with each door opening to a new dimension in awareness, understanding and knowledge of the Christ within. Let's examine each one.

Door No. 1: The Birth of Truth.

The primary work of the ancient teachings was the destruction of the old personality and the awakening of consciousness to the divinity of the individual. And one of the first activities was the planting of the seed of Truth. What Truth? The Idea that the Spirit of God is Man, the Spirit of Man is God, the Soul of Man is God in expression, and that Man is God made visible. Each man, each woman is a spiritual being, the very individualization of God. *You* are not a human being. You are God Being. . . and all of the powers of the universe are within you!

This was first taught in those ancient schools using the cosmos as a model, and later the initiations were based on the mystical lives of a Master or Savior. But it wasn't until Jesus walked this earth that the western world had a personal model on which to base the training for Christhood. At that point in history, the Idea of Truth became the Christ Idea, i.e. the Reality of you as an individual is the Christ, and when this seed of Truth is planted in consciousness, it begins to grow. And when it is accepted on the subjective side of your nature, you have gone through the process of being born again. This is the New

Birth represented in the Christmas story, and this Birth of Truth was what Jesus was referring to in his conversation with Nicodemus: "I say unto thee, except one be born anew, he cannot see the Kingdom of God."

The moment of recognition of the Truth of your Divinity is the moment of conception. Gestation follows, during which the Christ Idea develops in the soul and then comes forth (is born) in consciousness as awareness, understanding and knowledge of the indwelling Presence. But during the "pregnancy" great care must be taken to protect the new Life Form of Energy that is building and growing within the soul. The emotional nature (the mothering factor) must be continually fed with spiritual Truth, given rest from anger, fear and critical thoughts, and loved tenderly and gratefully. And then, in the fullness of time, the Child is born. You feel the Presence in your heart and you behold yourself as the Christ. . . God in individual expression. You are conscious of an indwelling Presence. This is the Babe who will overcome the world—your world—but again, it must be cared for and protected as it grows in strength and power.

At first the Child is weak and may seem to be asleep more than it is awake. But know this: with every degree of awakening, the greater the activity of God through you. . . so even the tiny Babe becomes a radiating center for Infinite Mind. And as the Christ Consciousness grows and waxes strong, it takes on **all Power**.

How does it feel to be born again? You know, because you have passed through this first door. Remember those feelings of excitement, joy and ecstasy? Recall the day your mind opened to behold new ways of living with peace, poise and power—and how you lifted your vision and saw yourself being and doing and having with no limitations. Are the feelings and vision still with you? Can you tune in and touch that Christ Vibration right now? If not, please go back and begin anew—get back to basics! Go back now to that first Door and experience the New Birth again.

Stop thinking about the unanswered prayers and the faulty demonstrations, or about the principles you thought you knew, or all the metaphysics you felt you had mastered. Start fresh and treat yourself to a good dose of Possibility Thinking! Recall the Truth that the Universe is *for* you...you are not just a victim of circumstances and a pawn of fate...you are a delightful Child of a Loving God and the only limitations you could ever have are the limitations you choose for yourself. Feel intuitively that all the Power of the Universe is within you, and through this Power you can rise above the gravity of mortal mind and mortal problems. Let the renewed awareness of your Victorious Self bring you out of the depths of lower mind vibration and lift you into a bright new world where all *good* things are possible. Plant the seeds of the Wholeness and Completeness of your True Self deeply in consciousness, and rest for a time from the pressures of the outer world. And as that Love Vibration begins to pulsate anew, you'll see the second Door standing before you.

Door No. 2: Escape from the Ego.

The Bible, that Codebook for metaphysicians and seekers of the Mysteries, talks about this door in the story of Joseph and Mary taking the infant Jesus into Egypt to escape the wrath of Herod. Herod signifies the ruling will of the sense consciousness, which seeks to destroy that which is spiritual because of the threat to its position of power. Egypt represents the place in deeper consciousness that temporarily harbors the Christ.

What this second Door means in our daily lives is that we must protect the Christ Truth while it is growing and developing in our consciousness, and the best way to do this is to "tell no man" after we have the New Birth experience. But this is against human nature. We have found a new joy and happiness and we want to tell everybody. Instead of hiding our new spiritual awareness and going daily into the silence until there is a greater understanding of principle, we have to tell everyone of our new Power. Rather than entering into a period of training our thoughts and emotions, we want to show everyone our stuff. And as we do, we blow the higher-vibration energy right out of our system.

I am not talking about the sharing of spiritual experiences with those of like mind, or verbal participation in classes on Truth, or the recommending of certain books to others seeking the Path. What I am referring to is indiscriminate talk about your spirituality, your demonstrations, and your new way of life to those of lower mind vibration. Don't cast your pearls unwisely. Let the energy building up around the Divine Idea become stabilized and secure. As the Christ Truth is protected and allowed to develop in the subconscious, a new vibration will come forth in your energy field and you will be given the key to the Third Door.

Door No. 3: Understanding the Law.

This particular initiation is symbolized in the story of Jesus in the temple at the age of 12, and his announcement of being about the Father's business. This is the first phase of spiritual adulthood, and it deals specifically with universal law — the law of cause and effect.

If you recall, Jesus was lost from his parents for three days — until they found him in the temple listening and talking to the teachers. This means that when we begin this initiation, we temporarily separate ourselves from the ideas of Love and Wisdom to prove that our understanding alone is sufficient to work with the law. But at this point, personal will is the motivating factor. The three days that Jesus was lost represent the first gathering together of mental, emotional and physical energies to make changes and produce results in the outer world. But the fourth part, the spiritual energy, has not been called into play as yet. And since we are "separated" from the primary power within at this time, we are engaging in a mental or mind treatment.

As we begin to mature in consciousness and start to understand the power we have, the first manifestation activity is almost always concentrated in mind and emotions. Our mental treatments include a great deal of affirmative prayer, treasure mapping, list making, visualizations, and speaking the word in *a third-dimensional consciousness*. Let's take an example. You may feel a sense of lack and limitation in your life. You know intellectually that this is not the reality of your being, so you attempt to change your consciousness from one of lack to one of abundance. You might affirm: "Wealth flows to me abundantly! The infinite intelligence of my subconscious mind attracts to me all the money I need to do everything I need to do."

Recognizing that you live in a thought world, you rationalize that in order to become rich and solve your financial problems, you must continuously dwell on thoughts of wealth, prosperity, and success—and you follow your affirmations with images of yourself being smothered with crisp, new bills and you speak the word: "Let there be wealth! Let there be abundance! Let money come forth now! Large sums of money are flowing into my life now! And it is so!"

Now remember that symbolically, you are "treating" this way at the age of 12, and while you may have reached the first stage of spiritual maturity, you are still working as an adolescent. But even an adolescent has power. Recall the temple story again. It said that "those who heard him were *astonished* at his powers." Those who were listening to Jesus were representative of the law—and they were astonished by his words. The root word of astonished is a connotation of extreme shock, a jarring, jolting impact. Now do you see what you have been doing with your third-dimensional treatments? Through your affirmations, visualizations and spoken word you have *shocked* your subjective nature. You have made a forceful contact, a penetrative impression which, by law, must be expressed. Since the mental treatment (example above) was for prosperity, you will have your prosperity demonstration...but it will not be lasting! "Mental" treatments without the spiritual connection do not result in lasting demonstrations because once your subjective mind recovers from the shock, it will revert back to its original vibration and you will be vulnerable again to experience limitation.

But every learning experience is good, so this stage devoted to mental treatments is simply part of the initiation to help you learn that the lower self can do nothing of a permanent nature. And the three days that you have been removed from the ideas of Love and Wisdom in consciousness also symbolize the time that is required for you to balance the will aspect of the mental, emotional and physical energies, and when that balancing takes place, you realize that you are lost without the spiritual side of your nature.

If we recall from the Jesus Model, we stay in this particular initiation (working with the law) for 18 years. That is a symbolic number, not a literal one. As Andrew Johnson (Quartus Research) discovered, "one" in Hebrew means ox, and carries the symbolism of desire, power and will. "Eight" in Hebrew means fence, and carries the meaning of a surrounding wall. The two together, 18, relate to the power of will to surround all of its activities with spiritual energy—to provide a safe place, a fortress, for spiritual growth while working with the law of cause and effect.

So, the time that is spent undergoing this initiation is in direct ratio to how quickly you can connect the four aspects of your being—the physical, emotional, mental and spiritual—while serving as a co-creator with God in working with the law. And to me, the secret of moving through this initiation is found in the words OF, AS, IS—where you work with the law as cause and not as an effect. You see, when you know that your consciousness _of_ God _as_ the fulfillment of any desire _is_ the fulfillment of that desire, you have a foundation for spiritual living—abundantly! Look at the code words in terms of supply, health, and relationships:

My consciousness _of_ God _as_ my supply _is_ my supply.

My consciousness _of_ God _as_ my health _is_ my health.

My consciousness _of_ God _as_ my perfect relationship _is_ my perfect relationship.

Fill in the blanks for your heart's desire:

My consciousness _of_ God _as_ my _____ _is_ my _____.

Let's break down the statement. First, "My consciousness _of_ God." This means your awareness, understanding and knowledge of the Presence within you—that God Presence, Christ, Spirit, Divine Mind, or whatever term for the Higher Power that is most comfortable for you. When you are aware of something, you draw that something into your awareness, which is your consciousness. And awareness leads to understanding, and understanding leads to knowledge.

When you turn your mind within and contemplate the Presence...when you focus on that Spirit within...when you recognize and become aware of the Infinite Mind right where you are, a most dramatic thing happens. At the moment of awareness, you literally open your consciousness to receive the Presence of God—because the energy, substance, intelligence, power, love and will of that Presence follows the beam of your awareness! Your entire energy field is filled with the very Spirit of God. Remember...God IS, but God is NOT in your experience unless there is awareness-recognition of the Presence. Spirit-Mind can express in your world only through your consciousness!

At this stage of your spiritual maturity, Spirit seems to ask you a question: "What would you have me be?" And that's why you must identify the Presence *as* that which you desire in the outer world. Let's say it is money. Money is a symbol of the Divine Idea of Supply, therefore, you must identify the Presence as your supply. Now let's connect the first two parts of the statement: "My consciousness *of* God *as* my supply." Your consciousness *of* God *as* your supply fills your consciousness with God as your supply. Therefore, your consciousness becomes your supply! We can now complete the statement: "My consciousness *of* God *as* my supply *is* my supply." Can you understand what happens when you embody the truth and meaning of that statement? Your consciousness becomes CAUSE to the outer world—and based on cosmic law, As Within, So Without.

Where do affirmations and visualizations come in? I like to think of affirmations as a way to correct my consciousness from a feeling of need to a sense of HAVE. Once you take on the God Energy and the Presence begins to act in your consciousness, you no longer feel that you have a selfhood apart from God. Your I AM is then God's I AM, and a simple affirmative statement such as "I am Abundance"—or—"I AM Health and Wholeness" is spoken with total assurance that you now HAVE abundance and health—even before the money and healing have become visible. And to visualize total fulfillment in every area of your life will keep the door open to the Light and provide a clear path for the Power to follow.

But the master key to this initiation is meditation ...contemplating and pondering the Presence within *as* your unlimited All. As you do this "without ceasing" you are *causing* changes to occur in the outer world. You have become the cause and the effects are appearing naturally. This is the secret message of this initiation: Become conscious of the Presence within as the fulfillment of any desire you have, and your consciousness will outpicture itself as that fulfillment...easily, quickly, and in peace.

Door No. 4: The Baptism.

When you enter the Fourth Door, you begin to purify the emotional nature and bring your heart and mind into alignment. As you do this, you will see that you'll never again be content with just good "humanhood."

Charles Fillmore wrote that "water baptism symbolizes a cleansing process, the letting go of error. It is the first step in the realization of truth." What is involved in the cleansing process? It is the giving up of everything that makes you feel less than divine, which means giving up all resentment, unforgiveness, fear, condemnation, prejudice, selfishness, guile, futility, deceit, irritation, rejection, etc., etc. It means spending time daily to purge your consciousness of all negative energy by forgiving all, loving all unconditionally, and letting the White Light pour through you to heal the error patterns and clear out the false beliefs. It means cutting the cord on every person, place and circumstance that makes you feel less than you are in Truth. It means taking control of your mind and emotions to see and sense and know and feel only the Truth—the Truth that *nothing* can touch you but the direct action of God and GOD IS LOVE!

If you have to go through the Baptism every single day for a year or a lifetime until it "takes"—then do it! Just because you are eternal does not mean you can put off achieving mastery forever.

Door No. 5: The Temptations.

As we follow the Jesus Model we see that the next door is the one leading to the Temptations, which vary across the board according to the vulnerability of each individual consciousness.

One temptation would be to fall back into the consciousness of using 3-dimensional forces to "make" something happen. It's a regressing back to the consciousness that says we have to coerce God into doing something for us — that we have to force God into meeting our needs or fulfilling our desires because of an unwillingness on God's part. Now you may say that you have grown beyond this type of thinking, but how many times have you faced a physical problem or a financial challenge and tried to fix the situation through mental work? People who do that are "metafixers" — not Metaphysicians. When you try to fix the outer world, you are concentrating on the effect and you are forgetting the Cause and shutting down the power. And you receive either a partial demonstration or no results at all, and the old ego says, "I told you so." You see, if the ego can lead you astray and tempt you to try something that fails, then you will think about giving up this spiritual work and get back down to working with him again — in the arena where he tries to be the boss.

Another temptation is to try to show off your spiritual power for personal glory. You may want to demonstrate a large sum of money, for example, to prove to others how spiritual you are — so you can tell everyone that they can have everything they want if they can just become as spiritually powerful as you are. And you rationalize this by thinking that you are proving a principle — that you are doing it for the glory of God. That kind of attitude is doomed to failure. While it is true that there are no limitations on what you can have, do, or be, just make sure that you don't try to manifest that fulfillment out of spiritual pride to call attention to yourself. If you do, you'll end up with a mouth full of ashes.

There is also the temptation to try to demonstrate beyond the range of your consciousness. Haven't you heard the ego say, "Don't worry about running up those charge accounts. . . Spirit will pay the bills when they come due." Or—"Why should you meditate to realize the Presence of God as your health? You take vitamins and jog don't you?"

But the greatest temptation is when the ego tries to influence us with emphasis on materiality rather than spirituality. And again, that means a concentration on the effect rather than the Cause. When you give power to an effect, you are giving it your power. You are actually giving the effect power over you. You *must* satisfy every need by steadfastly depending on the Master Self within, and not on anything in the outer world of form. This is really the meaning of the fifth initiation. . . the overcoming of the temptation to worship effects. . . where you take your stand and prove God now! As you do this, you'll find the Sixth Door opening.

Door No. 6: The Transmutation.

This door, or initiation, is symbolized by Jesus at the wedding party where he turned water into wine. And this is the door that launches us on the road toward service to mankind, because the soul is now telling us that we are ready to perform miracles. But we resist, saying that our time has not yet come. . . but the soul persists and alerts the chakras, the distributors of energy in our force field, to follow the orders of the personal I AM.

How many times have you found yourself in a negative situation, perhaps where you were not personally involved, and "something" within you said that you could harmonize the situation—that you have the power to transmute negativity into a positive experience? Your reaction was probably "I can't do anything about that." But the soul knows better and alerts the energy distributors (servants).

The Awakened Ones say that transmutation is based on the power of unconditional love, and we've written about this process in previous books. It's the idea that when you can love a situation with no strings attached (unconditionally), you can change the energy vibration that is holding the negative situation in place — that you can literally transmute a negative situation into a positive one. It is the idea of pronouncing something good regardless of how evil or ugly it looks, and then loving the goodness that is standing back of the illusion. And when you do this, the heart chakra opens and releases a super-powerful energy ray that dissolves the illusion and reveals the Reality.

When you are a bystander, it is frequently more interesting and stimulating to witness a negative situation rather than a positive one. Two men are fighting on the street corner and we pull over to watch. A man and woman are arguing at a table in a restaurant and we lean over to listen. Perhaps even Jesus was fascinated at all the people running around and wringing their hands because of the empty wine bottles.

But remember, you are here to be a healer and a harmonizer. No, you are **not** here to be a busy-body or a metafixer, nor are you to intrude in another's energy field or free-will process unless you are invited by the other person or through a genuine prompting from within. And you can tell if you are in the Sixth Zone and undergoing this particular initiation by the calls for help — from without or within. A friend drops by to discuss a challenge, and your soul prompts you to counsel him/her with unconditional love, correcting the error thought with Truth while radiating the Ray of Power Love to raise the consciousness vibrations of the individual. Later the friend calls you to say that the problem has completely disappeared. You have begun your miracle work.

And perhaps the next day you will be called upon to lay on hands and demonstrate your ability to be a channel for the healing power of Spirit. Or maybe you witness two factions opposing each other in your home, neighborhood, place of employment, or church — and you feel the urge from within to do your part to harmonize the situation, to transmute the negative energy. Without telling anyone what you are doing, you silently become a Secret Agent for God by radiating the Light and pouring unconditional Love into the situation. And as the vibrations of both groups are raised to the Divine

Standard, you will have seen still another "miracle."

Once you prove to yourself that you do indeed have the power to perform miracles, you are ready to enter the Seventh Door, where all of the power centers are opened and you prepare for world service.

Door No. 7: Gathering of the Powers.

This initiation is symbolized by the calling together of Jesus' disciples, with each "identity" representing one of the 12 powers of man. When these powers are awakened and begin to unite under the direction of the Superconsciousness, you will feel a balancing of your energy field — perhaps as never before.

In Charles Fillmore's book, *The Twelve Powers of Man*,[1] he writes: "The subconscious realm in man has twelve great centers of action, with twelve presiding egos or identities. When Jesus had attained a certain soul development, He called His twelve apostles to Him. This means that when man is developing out of mere personal consciousness into spiritual consciousness, he begins to train deeper and larger powers; he sends his thought down into the inner centers of his organism, and through his word quickens them to life. Where before his powers have worked in the personal, now they begin to expand and work in the universal."

The twelve powers are:

FAITH	UNDERSTANDING
STRENGTH	ENTHUSIASM
WISDOM	IMAGINATION
LOVE	ORDER
WILL	FORGIVENESS
AUTHORITY	LIFE

In *The Healing Secret of the Ages*,[2] Catherine Ponder looks at the twelve centers as healing powers, saying that "It is a teaching that has been well-guarded and was passed on from century to century to just a select few. It is a teaching that has remained a well-guarded secret even until this day. This secret teaching has to do with the 12 mind powers located within the vital nerve centers in your body. . . ."

Discussing the work of the ancient mystery schools in his book *The Theory of Celestial Influence*,[3] Rodney Collin writes: ". . . their (mystery schools) object must be to help a few suitable men to create conscious souls. One of the first things a man who becomes more conscious of himself and his surroundings will learn is that he cannot alter anybody; he can only alter his own point of view. And paradoxically, this understanding, if it really penetrates into him, immediately endows him with quite new powers and quite new freedom. This refers to the subjective acquisition of new powers through being freed from certain common illusions. But beyond this, increased consciousness may also bring objective powers, connected with the working of a new function through a hitherto unused nervous system. . . ."

Collin is pointing out that a major teaching of the schools was the development of forces residing in the subjective realm — to be used **consciously** by the individual in harmonizing his world. How are those "forces" developed? First of all, by understanding that the only person you can do anything about is yourself — that it is **your** consciousness that must be changed. Once you fully comprehend this, your focus begins to shift from without to within — to the discovery of your own power centers. And the energies of those centers are subsequently released and distributed throughout your multiple levels of being.

We call forth the powers by identifying with them and incorporating them into our I AM consciousness. Since the powers are already a part of our memory banks, we have them now — and remember that what we *have*, we can personalize. Accordingly, let's work with the awakening process in this manner:

Go into a meditative state and silently affirm each statement. Contemplate the idea behind the words for a minute or two, then speak the words aloud with great feeling.

I have Faith. It is a part of my being. It is what I am. I AM the Power of Faith. And I express that Power now!

I have Strength. It is a part of my being. It is what I am. I AM the Power of Strength. And I express that Power now!

I have Wisdom. It is a part of my being. It is what I am. I AM the Power of Wisdom. And I express that Power now!

I have Love. It is a part of my being. It is what I am. I AM the Power of Love. And I express that Power now!

I have Will. It is a part of my being. It is what I am. I AM the Power of Will. And I express that Power now!

I have Authority. It is a part of my being. It is what I am. I AM the Power of Authority. And I express that Power now!

I have Understanding. It is a part of my being. It is what I am. I AM the Power of Understanding. And I express that Power now!

I have Enthusiasm. It is a part of my being. It is what I am. I AM the Power of Enthusiasm. And I express that Power now!

I have Imagination. It is a part of my being. It is what I am. I AM the Power of Imagination. And I express that Power now!

I have Order. It is a part of my being. It is what I am. I AM the Power of Order. And I express that Power now!

I have Forgiveness. It is a part of my being. It is what I am. I

AM the Power of Forgiveness. And I express that Power now!

I have Life. It is a part of my being. It is what I am. I AM the Power of Life. And I express that Power now!

If you will work with this exercise daily, you will find an entirely new vibration pulsating in your energy field, freeing you from "common illusions" and endowing you with new powers and freedom. Then you will see the Eighth Door and will enter it with great eagerness.

Door No. 8: World Service.

By moving through the first seven initiations, or expansions in consciousness, we enter the Eighth Door and find ourselves with an understanding of our individual roles in serving humanity and the Divine Plan. Our concern is not group status or position, but what we can do to provide the greatest good to the greatest number of people without selfish motive or personal gain. The focus is simply on helping and serving others.

Sai Baba has this to say about service: "Do not judge others to decide whether they deserve your service. Find out only whether they are distressed; that is enough credential. Do not examine how they behave toward others; they can certainly be transformed by love. Service is for you as sacred as a vow ...it is the very breath; it can end only when breath takes leave of you."[4]

And the Tibetan Master, D.K., has written: "(The) Law of Service was expressed for the first time fully by the Christ two thousand years ago. Today, we have a world which is steadily coming to the realization that 'no man liveth unto himself,' and that only as the love, about which so much has been written and spoken, finds its outlet in service, can man begin to measure up to his innate capacity."[5]

What is your service? Through meditation the inner Voice will reveal your "piece of the puzzle" — but while you're listening, also begin to take action. Here are a few suggestions:

1. Set up a regular schedule of spiritual activities, including specific periods of meditation and a time to work with your spiritual exercises. Plan your time, and if necessary, get up earlier each morning. Remember, the upliftment of your consciousness is your Number One priority!

2. Attend the church of your choice regularly and participate in its activities. Get involved in a Wednesday evening class, a Course in Miracles group, a Quartus study group, or other such gatherings—and share your understanding, love and energy for the benefit of all.

3. Reach out to others on the Path and help in everyway you can. Sometimes just listening to another's story of pitfalls on the journey can help him or her release the negative energy—then join with that person in affirmative prayer and meditation to open the door to greater understanding for both of you.

4. Be a healing influence for this world, beginning right in your own home and place of work. Remember..."Let there be peace on earth and let it begin with **me**." Use the power of will (purpose of mind) to open your heart chakra and radiate love to heal every negative situation you see. Be a Secret Agent for God and use your Lasers (Love Activated Spiritual Energy Rays) to melt illusions of discord and reveal the Reality of Harmony.

5. Take a definite action every single day to spread the Word of Light, Love, Peace, Good Will, Forgiveness, and Understanding. Write a letter; gather signatures for the Planetary Commission; talk about the world-wide meditation on December 31, 1986; share the Healing Meditation with someone; give a friend a spiritual book; take someone to church; participate in a gathering; pick up the phone and call a person who needs your encouragement; share your supply under the guidance of Spirit; smile more, touch more, heal more, do more, be more!

Remember...the salvation of the world really does depend on **you**!

Door No. 9: The Transfiguration.

In the *Metaphysical Bible Dictionary*[6] we read, "According to Mark 9:2-13, 'Jesus went up into a mountain to pray, and was there transfigured.' Prayer always brings about an exalted or rapid radiation of mental energy, and when it is accompanied by faith, love and wisdom — represented by Peter, John and James — there is a lifting up of the soul that electrifies the body...the aura surrounding the body shines with glistening whiteness."

The transfiguration is not something you make happen. It comes naturally when your meditations, treatments and prayers have moved beyond work on your own behalf and have become more universal in scope. You see, when you move beyond yourself and begin to work spiritually as a member of the planetary family on behalf of that family, the energy of the lower nature begins to rise...and then one day or night, during or following deep meditation when you are radiating love and light to this world, a reuniting of your lower and higher natures takes place. The natural and the divine are integrated...the personality and individuality are unified...a metamorphosis takes place and you are filled with light. Those who have not experienced the transfiguration cannot express it in words. It is a moment of illumination, the body feels electrified, and the aura does indeed shine "with glistening whiteness."

In *The Planetary Commission* I relate an experience of transfiguration as reported by one of our Quartus members:

"For several hours while my husband watched in awe, I appeared transformed. I experienced the most ecstatic, intense, beautiful love. I was truly one with God and the Universe. I was part of everything and everything was a part of me. The trees glowed, their green was greener; the buildings were brighter; the air was fresher; everything and everyone was perfect and beautiful. Eventually I went back to normal again, except that I became closer to God than ever before, and that closeness has never left me. My fear of death was also gone."

What can you do to open this Ninth Door and insure the transfiguration experience? Set your sights on service! Ask yourself everyday: "What can I do for my fellowman? How can I be of greater service to others? What can I do for this world?" And consider the answer in terms of activity on both the spiritual and physical planes — spiritually with prayer and meditation on behalf of others and this planet, and physically with direct action in expressing your piece of the puzzle. And as the focus moves beyond the personal you and becomes more universal, the metamorphosis will take place and the realization of your divinity will flow through you like an electric shock!

Door No. 10: The Crucifixion.

What is the crucifixion? It is the sacrifice of the integrated lower nature. The lower self, even though redeemed now, must die in order for the Higher Self to fully manifest. It is the giving up of the personality. . .a replacing of the human consciousness with the divine consciousness. It is a crossing out of both the objective and subjective planes of consciousness. But you, personally, will have little to do with the crucifixion. . .it will truly be the Father within who will doeth the work.

A strange, yet wonderful, experience takes place at the crucifixion. Since the transfiguration, you have been operating out of a higher vibration consciousness *of* the Christ within. . .a firm and strong awareness *of* the Christ Spirit, an understanding *of* the nature of that Spirit, and a knowledge *of* your relationship with Spirit. But at the crucifixion, this awareness and comprehension begins to fade out as the personal consciousness takes on the identity of its Source. There is a fading out of one consciousness and a fading in of another — but for a short period in between, the feeling of the Presence leaves you and you may well cry out, "My God, my God, why hast thou forsaken me?" But as the full understanding of your divinity takes place, the "I and the Father are one" becomes a complete realization. At that moment, the Eleventh Door opens.

Door No. 11: The Resurrection.

Now you live and move and have your being *as* the Christ. The Spirit in man has been crucified and now only Christ lives and you fully demonstrate the Truth of your Being.

There are 40 days from the resurrection to the ascension, or the entering of the Twelfth Door. "Forty" is symbolic of preparation, so there is further work to be done before the final initiation. And the primary objective of this work is to verify the claim that spiritual man is all powerful, and that the crucifixion means life and not death.

While I realize that there are varying degrees of crucifixion that we all go through in the many stages of our evolvement, the final crossing out of humanhood and the resurrection of the Christ within brings an individual to the beginning of total mastery. And there are risen Christs all over this planet today...men and women who have spiritualized their bodies, their emotions and their minds, and who have total dominion over the so-called material or physical planes of existence.

From the knowledge of these masters we know that more than 500-million men and women are between the Fourth Door (Baptism) and the Tenth Door (Crucifixion)—and more than 50-million have gone through the crucifixion and have been resurrected into the Christ Consciousness. And, according to the awakened one called Jason Andrews in *The Superbeings*, there are several hundred Earth Masters, those who have gone through the Ascension initiation, living on our planet today.

Before we can enter that 12th Door and the initiation of Ascension, there are ten duties to perform, according to the Jesus Model. And these duties are based on his ten appearances after the Resurrection. You can read about the ten appearances in your Bible, but the symbolism of the work you must do once you attain Christhood is as follows: (Do them now by playing the role of the Christ, and the Resurrection experience will be yours sooner than you think.)

1. You must minister to those whom you are the closest, to teach the principle of detachment so that they may release

themselves from all attachments, including you. There can be no sense of possessiveness in or around spiritual consciousness. This does not mean that anyone loves less. Quite the contrary. There is deeper and greater love because it is unconditional... no strings attached.

2. You are to teach by thought, word and example that there is nothing to fear in this world — that anything that we could possibly fear is but an illusion.

3. You are to help others release the Power of Faith... faith in the invisible Presence within.

4. You are to share the truth you know with all true believers in the divinity of man — to help others awaken to their divinity.

5. You are to call forth the Spirit of Wholeness, the Holy Spirit, in every single individual you encounter. Silently salute the divinity within each man, woman and child. Call forth the Christ in all.

6. Through your thoughts, words and deeds, you are to contribute to the spiritual understanding of others, the understanding of God, of man.

7. You are to share with others the principle of abundance... the truth that God is the Source of all supply, that the consciousness of this truth *is* their supply because this consciousness manifests as visible supply.

8. You are to give a commission to those who love the indwelling Christ to go into the world to spread the good news that Christ lives within each heart — that the resurrection of the Christ within is the salvation of each individual and the world.

9. You are to let Divine Wisdom be the guiding light in everything you think, say and do.

10. You are to work in the vibration of total unconditional love, and through that Love Power to assist others in transmuting negative energy, false beliefs and error patterns so that the very Spirit of God, the Holy Spirit, may descend into their consciousness.

This is your work as a spiritual master in your own community, and through these activities you will have prepared yourself for the Twelfth Door.

Door No. 12: The Ascension.

When you move through this door, you become an Earth Master. Your will is totally merged with the Will of God, and you are now a radiating Center for the Good Will of God.

The first eight doors are opened by us...the final four are opened by Spirit. How far we go to where Spirit takes over depends on our choice, our decision, our commitment.

After all, we do have the gift of free will.

10

Questions and Answers

Q: What is karma?

A: Karma is the law of cause and effect in operation through the volition of the individual, i.e. where a choice or decision is involved. If the choice — through thought, word or deed — is based on the principle of good-for-all, good karma is impressed in the Akashic Records. However, if the mental-emotional-physical action is negative, it is etched as a "print" or pattern of negative energy in the Records. This negative pattern will continually influence your life and affairs until it is corrected or worked out.

The vibration of your energy field at this moment comes from both your self-created positive and negative karmic patterns. Those patterns are reinforced by drawing like energy from other individuals (like attracts like). Accordingly, a high-vibration consciousness (good karma) will attract those who will help you achieve your goals, and you will be drawn to those whom you can provide loving assistance. But a heavy karmic wheel loaded with debts created through negative actions will attract rather unpleasant people and experiences into your life—and your negative energy will be taken on by others of a similar vibration. And this negative attraction will help you to work out your karmic debts on the physical plane.

Understand that every karmic debt left unpaid when you make your transition will be carried over to another life. So isn't it foolish to go through your days in this incarnation bogged down with the patterns of your miscreations, and then having to bring them all back with you again? The negative energy pulsating in your force-field makes you vulnerable to just about every type of undesirable condition—and you can satisfy your debts by experiencing those conditions. But never forget...*you* are the master of your destiny, and you can neutralize those patterns and transmute the negative energy. How? By making a definite decision, a choice through your will, to think, feel, speak and act according to the Christ standard. Forgive yourself and forgive all others without exception. Take control of your thoughts and correct your thinking the instant it tilts downward. Cancel out negative feelings by practicing unconditional love with everyone. Watch your words and speak only words for creative and progressive good. Consider the motive behind every action and make sure that you will create only good for yourself and others. And above all, spend time each day in silent contemplation of, and meditation on, the Spirit of God within you. As you realize the Presence and assume your true Identity, the slate will be wiped clean and you will be free.

Q: Please explain "chemicalization" for me. Does it relate to the ego?

A: Let's look first at the definition of *chemistry*: "A science that deals with the composition, structure and properties of substances and of the transformation that they undergo." Now to give you a simple illustration of the transformation of structure, take a bottle, add some dirt, fill it with water, and let it sit for a period of time. Notice that the dirt has settled to the bottom. Now take the bottle and shake it and watch what happens. This is precisely the experience of many people who embark on a study of Truth and the awakening of consciousness. The new seeds of Truth planted in consciousness may "shake up" your energy field and bring all of the old karmic patterns to the surface. And this altered vibration may attract a multitude of unsettling experiences into your life.

How often we have heard—"Everything in my life seemed to fall apart when I began my spiritual journey." To say that this is all a part of the cleansing process may not seem very comforting, but that's what it is all about. Also, as I pointed out in the "No Man's Land" chapter in *The Planetary Commission*, taking steps to lose the identify of the lower self and awaken to the divinity of your Higher Self can be a real threat to the ego—and it will do whatever it can to show who is boss, even if that means causing a few rockslides on your path.

In *Lessons in Truth*,[1] Emilie Cady talks about chemicalization this way: (It occurs when) "there has been a clash between the old condition—which was based on falsehood, fear and wrong ways of thinking—and the new thought of truth entering into you. The old mortal is kicking vigorously against the truth. This agitation does not always take place with everyone, but is most apt to occur with those who have been most fixed, as it were, solidified in the old beliefs. Such people break up with more resistance."

Q: You seem to not favor the idea of listening to tapes that help to impress the subconscious with truth ideas. Why not?

A: It is the exclusive use of such tapes that bother me, and I guess it's because I feel that too much emphasis has been placed on "programming" the subconscious with outer stimuli. This leads a person to believe that he can only be whole (in body, pocketbook and relationships) if he can make his subconscious believe that this is so. To me, this is denying our innate wholeness. If I am constantly affirming that I am rich, then I must "secretly" believe that I am not. I will agree that the subconscious must be brought into alignment with the Truth of our being, but the Soul or Superconsciousness is much more effective in doing that than anyone's conscious mind. So, I suggest that you turn over the "impression making" to the Master within. And meditation is the way.

Q: I have heard that Quartus has a "Prosperity Checklist." Would you please share it?

A: Ask yourself:
( ) Is my primary interest in realizing the Presence of God, or is it in meeting a financial problem?
( ) Am I still concentrating on the effect (money), or am I focusing my attention on Cause (Spirit)?
( ) Am I willing to take my stand now and prove God once and for all as my all-sufficiency?
( ) Have I devoted the necessary time to meditating on the Spirit within as the Source of my prosperity?
( ) Am I conscious of the inner Presence as my abundance?
( ) Do I have the understanding that my consciousness of the Presence is my supply?
( ) Am I trying to demonstrate money, or develop a greater consciousness of abundance?
( ) Have I accepted the Truth that the living Presence within me is my all-sufficiency, and that the activity of this Infinite Mind is meeting my every need at this moment?
( ) Have I identified myself with my all-sufficient Self so that I can say with great conviction "I AM Abundance?"
( ) Knowing that my consciousness of the indwelling Presence is my supply, can I now affirm and believe the Truth that I *have* abundance?
( ) Can I see myself fulfilled and enjoying lavish abundance in my life and affairs?
( ) Have I truly expressed a feeling of love for the visions of wholeness and completeness that I see in my visualizations?
( ) Do I intuitively feel that Spirit *has* manifest as my

all-sufficiency even though the results may still be invisible? Have I spoken the word that "It is done?"

( ) Have I totally surrendered all my needs, desires, fears and concerns to the Presence within?

( ) Have I expressed a deep sense of gratitude to the Spirit within *before* my good comes forth into visible manifestation? Is my heart overflowing with thankfulness and joy the majority of my waking hours?

( ) Am I listening to the Voice within for guidance and instructions regarding any action that I am to take in the outer world? Am I following through with that action?

( ) Have I totally forgiven everyone and everything in my consciousness?

( ) Am I practicing unconditional love with everyone in my life?

( ) Have I maintained a state of secrecy regarding the use of spiritual principles in the demonstration of my supply?

( ) Knowing the Reality within all and the Truth about all, can I see everyone on this planet as abundantly supplied with every good thing, regardless of appearances?

( ) Do I desire for everyone else that which I desire for myself?

( ) Am I a joyful giver? Do I freely share my money on a regular basis, knowing that as I give, so shall I receive, pressed down and running over?

( ) Have I done all that I can do to improve my relationship with my children?

( ) In my personal relationship with my mate or love partner, do I care more about his/her feelings and welfare than I do my own?

( ) Am I working to overcome any problems related to sex in my life?

( ) Am I involved in a meaningful activity for creative self-expression?

( ) Am I working on my Life Plan to see myself as whole and complete in every area of my life?

The more questions you have answered with a "YES" — the richer you are in mind *and* manifestation.

Q: You mentioned in The Superbeings that Quartus was forming a Council of Masters. Have you done this?

A: The objective during the early stages of Quartus was to attract as many men and women as possible with an illumined or awakened spiritual Consciousness, and to encourage input from these people on a variety of subjects. As far as we can determine, approximately 10 percent of the membership represents those who have taken on the Christ Vibration and have risen above humanhood. However, we have found that they are much too busy with their spiritual work on behalf of humanity to constantly answer questions submitted to them. It is interesting, though, that we frequently receive letters and other materials from them, and in these writings we find new ideas, insights and understanding. So, we do have a "council" — even though it is informal and unstructured. To this group of physical men and women we should add the guides who work with us, and we should mention that the "Chairperson" of the group is the Christ Spirit within us all.

Understand that the communications from Quartus are not to represent the teaching of one man or woman. Through contributions of concepts and truth interpretations from those on the physical plane, combined with understanding gained from the realm of Soul/Spirit, we seek to develop a fund of knowledge to be shared with those who are interested. And the purpose for this is NOT to develop your consciousness so that in time you may be brought to a Master who can then lead you to Cosmic Consciousness. No, it's just the other way around. Our objective is to assist you in opening the door to your own Soul so that the one Master Teacher within you may be realized and experienced.

Q: I have been told that the time of our death is predetermined. Is this true?

A: There are esoteric teachings that say that prior to each incarnation the soul chooses three times/situations/

occurrences in which transition may take place, and these are spaced out over a life span. As the first exit opportunity nears, a deeper-than-conscious phase of mind will either consent or dissent, based on whether or not the soul's priority has been met. If not, the physical life continues to the next "opening" and another evaluation is made. If, for one reason or another, the next or third opportunity is also passed up, then a conscious choice (a call to return) will be issued by the soul at a later time. This final "exiting" will be in accordance with the impersonal law of cause and effect, using the most appropriate opportunity based on the patterns in consciousness, i.e. that which we fear the most will be drawn to us.

We must also understand that the body does not live or die. . . it only reflects consciousness. And I firmly believe that as we tune the vibration of consciousness to Spirit—and maintain that High Vibration—we can keep the body with us as long as we desire, right up to the moment of translation.

Fern Hook, minister of the Christ Today Healing and Teaching Ministry in Lake Elsinore, California, has expressed deep insights into the translation experience in her monthly Letters[2] to students. In her July 1985 Letter she writes: ". . .there are certain divine principles that the reasoning mind finds very difficult to accept. Among those is the premise that God did not create physical birth and death. Because it has always appeared that mankind is destined to die, and is subject to the patterns of nature—the material body being so much like the forms in animal life—there has not been an acceptance of the possibility of ascension out of the mortal body, even though it has been demonstrated by certain evolved souls all through the ages.

"Many translations were recorded and vouched for, but were not given credence. They were kept secret because they were not the normal experience, and the analyzing mind had many reasons that such a thing would not be possible. The same arguments are presented today. For example, one of the first questions regarding translation from physical form to immortal form is 'How can this planet support so many people if there is no death?' The answer to that is simple. Conquering physical death includes the elimination of physical birth. If we do not die, we will have no mortal births and will be finished with reincarnating. Translation is not just an extension of physical life; it is rather the beginning of a life of freedom to roam the universes that are composed of different levels of consciousness and form!"

Q: What does the "Will of God" mean?

A: We know that "will" is defined as strength of purpose, determination, resolution, desire. In the Mind of God, "Will" means the Cosmic Urge to express—the desire to manifest Perfection in, as, and through Its creations. Consider, too, that the will of God is the vision of God and the action fulfilling that vision. In other words, Spirit sees only Perfection, therefore only Perfection is expressed.

This is why the ancients said to "put an end to praying." Yet we are also told to "pray without ceasing." Both statements are correct when properly interpreted. The first one is based on the truth that there is nothing to pray for because God has already given us everything. We have been given the Kingdom, which represents the Spirit of God within us. Jesus called the Presence "Father." Paul called it "Christ." Whatever you call it, it is still the same—your God Self. And this Self, this Spirit within you has nothing to give you. It cannot give you health because it **is** Health. It cannot give you abundance because it **is** Abundance. So you see, when you pray for health or abundance, you are praying amiss, because you already *have* all the health, the wellness, the perfection, the abundance, the prosperity, the supply there is. You are already whole and complete, for that is the will of God! And since the will of God is eternally fulfilled, nothing can be added to you...there is nothing for you to "get"....all you can do is *release* that which you already have and let it come forth into visibility.

How do we let Spirit appear as every needed thing? That's where "praying without ceasing" comes in. When we meditate on the Presence within as the fulfillment of every desire. . . when we become aware of our spiritual Reality and contemplate the Truth of our Being, we open the healing channel and reconnect the supply line and the link between heaven and earth is again established. At that point the will of God can be expressed on earth as it is in heaven, and our lives are transformed according to the Higher Vision of Spirit.

During your meditations you should surrender the will of ego to Spirit with the declaration "Not my will, but Thine be done." When you let go and hand over your personal will to the Power within, the creative activity (will) of Spirit will be released to prosper your affairs, heal your body, establish your divine work, and bring the right people into your life. When you practice the Presence of your God Self and consciously surrender to the activity of that Self, marvelous and miraculous things will happen in your life. And the reason will be because you have stopped trying to make something happen. You are finally willing to accept your highest good! Please understand that the activity of God's will *always* results in greater joy and happiness than you could possibly conceive from your third-dimensional perspective.

As Ernest Holmes has written, "The will of God for you is the will of a boundless life, flowing through you. It is the will of joy, of success, of happiness, of peace, of abundance."[3]

Q: How does "absent healing" work?

A: Ask a group of healers and the answer will be much the same: "God is the Source of all healing. . .I simply clear the channel for His work." This "clearing the channel" means that the patient's energy field has been sufficiently raised in vibration to activate the healing currents. And the process in doing this varies among the healers. At Quartus, for example, one particular individual receives the name and location of the person needing the healing, establishes a link in consciousness with that person for several minutes, then goes into meditation to "treat" the patient by realizing his (the healer's) own perfect Self. As the healer makes contact with his own God Presence within, the healing energies are projected directly to the patient to stimulate the healing process. And it does not make any difference whether the problem has been physical, financial, the need for a relationship, a threatening job situation, or whatever.

Another healer frequently projects herself into the patient's energy field, and radiates love with great intensity to develop a receptivity to the healing currents from the patient's own Higher Self.

Some rely on the spoken word, decreeing the Truth about the individual and continuing with the treatment until there is an inner feeling that the work is done, while others simply transmit their high level of spiritual consciousness to the patient. Still others work with a form of the "manifestation process" — but all treat from the vantage point of seeing only the Truth of the individual, i.e. focusing only on the spiritual Self, which is now and always has been perfect.

We also have records of many healings from people who have called Silent Unity, or who have been treated spiritually by a Religious Science or Divine Science practitioner. In each case it was the activity of the Christ Consciousness taking place within those individuals receiving the healing request.

Why are some healed while others are not? I believe that the answer lies in the letting go or surrendering process. If there is any doubt involved, or if there is an attitude of holding back and not fully giving up the challenge, the necessary connection in consciousness will not be made and the individual may not benefit. We must also understand that each one of us has an electromagnetic shield. If we truly desire a healing, the shield will permit the cleansing Light to enter and raise the vibration. However, if an individual has chosen, perhaps on the subconscious level, to work through a problem without the assistance of others in order to master a lesson, he will "shield" himself from the positive influences.

One further point. Some people greatly desire a healing but are inhibited for one reason or another from asking for help. One young man told me that he didn't reach out for assistance because he wanted to heal himself. That's fine unless it's ego talking. Healing *is* a do-it-yourself project when we have the proper consciousness for it. In fact, we all are to become so transparent to Spirit that all challenges disappear through the activity of the Presence within. But as we're going through the awakening process, if we need help let's ask for it! Just know that requesting assistance with challenges does not make you appear any less spiritual.

Q: Do pets have souls?

A: I was so glad when the letter asking this question came in, because it gave me the opportunity to tell the Maggi story again. (It was originally included in the December 1983 edition of the Quartus Report.)

The story begins on the evening of July 17, 1981. Jan and I had finished dinner and were watching a movie on television. It wasn't a sad show, but suddenly tears started rolling down my cheeks and my heart became so heavy that I had to get up and go outside. Jan knew something was wrong, but said nothing, knowing that when I was ready to talk about it I would. I sat down on the grass in the backyard beside our dog Brandy—a 10-year old Springer Spaniel who was as much a part of our lives as our very own children. For more than an hour I sat there and bawled like a baby, with a sadness unlike anything I had ever experienced. When I finally went back into the house, I really had nothing to tell Jan, because I had no idea why I had been so grief-stricken. It wasn't until the next morning that I knew.

While we were having breakfast that next day, Brandy was on the floor between us—and we both noticed that she was having difficulty breathing. She had been sick off and on for about three months, and we had taken her to the vet several times for various medications. And of course, we had worked with her spiritually, but in looking back, this kind of treatment was done much too casually. Anyway, we picked her up and drove to the vet as quickly as possible, but within minutes after our arrival she died. Then I knew what I had been "told" the night before—and the grief came back like a tidal wave, engulfing both of us. Oh how we cried! And the tears flowed for the rest of the day and into the night...and the next morning there was still no relief.

During meditation on Sunday, which I found extremely difficult to get into, something quite unexpected happened. All of a sudden Brandy appeared right in front of me, saying "Lift up your vision." I was startled—and the first thought that came into my mind was *don't judge by appearances*.

Then, two nights later I had a dream. I could see Brandy through a thin curtain. I was on one side and she was on the other, and she was trying desperately to claw her way through. I woke up, shook Jan and told her that we must release Brandy at once...that our grief was holding her from her highest good. So we spoke the word to let her go, and with very wet eyes went back to sleep.

A week later, an unusual sequence of dreams began—each about a week apart. In the first one I was walking down a country road and Brandy came running up beside me, saying "Tell Mommy I'm coming back." And I said (for some strange reason), "That's not her name, her name is Jan." Brandy replied: "But you always called her Mommy in front of me." Then she ran off down the road. I didn't say anything to Jan the next morning. After all, it was only a dream.

In the second dream, I was walking down that same country road and here comes Brandy again, almost hollering this time: "You didn't tell Mommy that I'm coming back." I just smiled at her, and she said again, "You'd better tell her because I'm coming back on October 20th."

Well, you can imagine what happened when the alarm went off the next morning. I said, "Jan, I've got something to tell you...something a bit strange, but I've been told that I'd *better* tell you." Then I reviewed both dreams. Jan just looked at me with those big brown eyes and didn't say anything.

Then about a week later I had the third dream. This time I am leaning against a fence talking to Brandy (can't remember that particular conversation) and another Springer Spaniel runs up. I lean down to pat her and Brandy says, "Be careful, she's four years old." And I asked, "What does that mean?" And she replied, with a big grin on her face, "You'll know."

In the next dream we were walking down that country road again, talking like two old friends. (She was walking upright and was as tall as I was.) She said, "By the way, I'm changing my consciousness this time." I stopped, looked right in her eyes and asked, "But why? I love you the way you are!" She responds: "Oh, I'll still be the same dog, the same soul, but I don't want to have another heart attack, so I am changing my consciousness." I said, "I understand."

In dream number five she tells me to "look for the white!" And when I ask what that means, she just grins and says, "You'll know." And in the final dream she is very emphatic in saying, "Don't try to find me. Don't do anything. It's all been worked out, so don't run around looking for me. You'll know!"

After Brandy left us in July, I wrote the final chapter in *The Superbeings* — "The Ultimate Way" — and made preparations for the printing of the book.

In September, our daughter Susan moved from Houston to Austin, bringing her huge cat with her, and moved in with us until she could find her own apartment. When she arrived, Jan noticed a deep scratch on the cat and suggested that "Puff" be taken to the vet. While she and Susan were there the vet asked, "Jan, are you and John ready for another dog yet?" Jan, being very cautious, said "I don't know...we'll just wait and see." And the vet said, "Well, if you decide you want another Springer, here's the name and telephone number of a woman whose dog is going to have a litter." Jan took the information and that night called the woman. After checking us out in what seemed like an FBI investigation, Jan was finally able to ask, "When are the pups due?" The woman answered, "October 20th." We got goose bumps. The woman then said, "And this is my Springer's first litter." Jan asked, "How old is your dog?" The reply, "Four years old."

We were right on target at this point, but we couldn't do anything else until the pups were born. ("Look for the white," she had said.) But just as soon as we heard that the baby Springers had arrived, Jan and I were kneeling over the box. . . and right in the middle of the litter was a little female with huge white patches over a background of liver-brown. (Brandy had been almost all brown.) We immediately put in our claim for *that* one, and visited her constantly until we could bring her home.

Brandy always had an unusual way of greeting us. She would sit down on her haunches and raise her two front paws in the air — in almost a "take me I'm yours" kind of posture. When the new pups were four weeks old, we visited them on a Sunday afternoon and they were all out playing in the grass. As we got out of the car and walked across the lawn, the little white and brown one turned, saw us coming, managed to get up on her little rear end and held her paws up high — just like Brandy used to do. This almost did Jan in, and she ran across the yard squealing "My baby, my baby!"

When we brought her home at six weeks, she telepathically told us that she wanted a new name (we had considered calling her Brandy again). So after discussing various names, she decided on "Magnificent Brandy Too" — and we call her Maggi for short. And yes, she has that same gentle, loving, joy-filled personality that she displayed before. And she continues to teach us so much. . . including a special reverence for all life, and the Truth that a soul never dies. . . not even a dog. . . especially not a dog!

EPILOGUE

This book was already in the typesetting stage when a stream of thoughts came through one morning during meditation. I jotted them down and decided to add an Epilogue.

The "flow-through" dealt with the word **dominion**. "...let them have dominion...over the earth..." (Gen. 1:26) What does dominion mean? It is defined as one having authority, sovereignty, mastery. It also means stewardship — the management of earthly concerns and needs. However, if we look at the situation on the planet today, we may wonder what happened to our mastery and our ability to manage. To find the answer let's refer to the Bible again and look at Genesis 1:27 — "So God created man in his own image, in the image of God created he him; male and female created he them." And in Verse 28: "And God blessed them, and God said unto them, Be fruitful, and multiply and replenish the earth, and subdue it; and have dominion over...every living thing that moveth upon the earth."

From your understanding you know that this was Spiritual Man who was blessed and given dominion, not the third-dimensional physical man. The Soul of that man wasn't even formed out of Cosmic Energy until the six stages of creation and the "cycle of rest" were completed, as recorded in Genesis 2, Verse 7. So we see that mastery and stewardship were given to the Image of God, and I AM, our Spiritual Reality. Therefore, if we want to claim and use the dominion-power to replenish the earth and subdue (which means to reduce intensity) the forces of nature, we must realize our oneness with the Self who was given dominion in the first place. What happens then? Can we really make a difference in this world by taking on that higher vibration? Let's answer these questions by looking at the dominion process from a very practical standpoint.

Let There Be Light!

We are told that each individual being is the "Light of the World"—and that the Power of the Light is within us. We have also been referred to as Lightbearers and Light Beings. What does this mean? Scientists tell us that light is *energy* producing hundreds of trillions of vibrations per second in the form of light waves. Consider now that the Source of Light is within you and that light waves are eternally emanating from your consciousness, radiating as *lines of force*. These lines of force govern electrons (the electrical charges whirling around the nucleus of atoms) and cause atoms to cluster in an energy field as a thought form. This energy configuration is then "stepped down" through levels of substance to become visible on the physical plane.

Everything considered "matter"—whether visible or invisible—is made up of atoms, or pure energy. Therefore, everything seen and unseen is energy in motion, and this *energy of everything* is controlled by thought. The consciousness of the individual is the transmitter of energy and the directing force that destroys or creates form and experience. Contemplate this!

The lines of force radiate from centers of High Vibration or low vibration, depending on the frequency of consciousness. You are either healing or harming...there is no inbetween. You can see now why the purity of thought based on the at-one-ment principle is of vital importance. In our present world, there is much negative energy controlling the lines of force, thus creating a disruption of the natural balance of atoms and causing conflicting patterns in the mineral, plant, animal and human kingdoms, and on both the physical and etheric planes.

As long as negative thought energy is the major influence on the lines of force, there will continue to be a *deterioration* of everything visible. And the actual renewal of all aspects of planetary life will not begin until we reach the point where the positive exceeds the negative, i.e. 51% on a scale of 1 to 100. At that point, when the scales are tipped in favor of constructive spiritual energy, things will begin to happen in our world of a positive nature. Through the Light of Spirit radiating from within and moving into the third-dimensional plane, the pattern of the movement of electrons will be changed and the atomic structure of matter altered, including every "force" on earth. Yes, *your* high-vibration consciousness can affect wind, fire, water, land, and the very air we breathe.

Is there any evidence that this is true? Definitely yes! Through the radiation aspect of meditation, and the altering force of energy liberated through creative visualization and the spoken word, the "outer picture" can be changed. We know from scientific studies that meditation affects the first visible manifestation of organized atoms, i.e. the physical body. While in meditation the electrical activity of the brain synchronizes and brings balance and harmony to brain waves that have been out of phase and on different frequencies. The result: a higher level of intelligence and creativity. Meditation also normalizes the nervous system and causes many physiological changes that are of great benefit to the physical system.

As we move beyond the body we see beneficial changes continuing to take place. Those individuals who regularly practice the art of meditation and have achieved a degree of spiritual consciousness find protection from, or dominion over, destructive forces and negative circumstances. And in the Quartus files of member experiences, there are many instances where the spoken word and/or visualization have changed the course of tornadoes, protected home and property from a forest fire, held back floods, stopped rain, protected crops during a freeze, prevented an airplane crash, restored plant life, multiplied provisions to alleviate a food shortage, manifested visible money supply, protected life and property from crime, and brought forth "miraculous" escapes from accidents. Don't tell me that the spiritual life isn't practical!

In most cases, these experiences were based on the release of Light by a single individual. There are also documented reports of group experiments with meditation resulting in substantial drops in homicides, suicides, and accidents in the test communities. And in our group meditations at Quartus, the "unified field" theory has been tested with excellent results — as evidenced by the healings in mind, body, relationships, employment, and supply.

So we see that Spirit Light not only eliminates the dark forces created by mortal mind, which are manifesting as the destructive power of nature, but also rearranges atomic substance and creates new forms and experiences according to the spiritual counterpart-body of nature and the planet. The Light within you and me is the form-building energy of all manifestation! By tuning into the vibration of the Divine Self, and then by using our minds as radiating centers, we literally create a force field that begins to work on the etheric level to transmute negative energy and reveal the Reality that has always been behind the illusion. This is the function and purpose of the Lightbearers, the Light Beings, that which we are in truth.

It all begins with individual you and me moving into spiritual consciousness, filling our minds with spiritual energy, thinking spiritual thoughts, visualizing spiritual healing and harmony, speaking the spiritual word — all of which will activate the *right* lines of force, and the chain reaction of good begins.

This brings us full circle to the original point of this Epilogue: *Dominion*. We have seen that individual men and women are working with the Cosmic Light to heal and harmonize their immediate environment. And we have seen what groups can do when the Light is focused to reveal Reality in particular situations. Now...since we have evidence that we can make positive changes in the outer picture, why isn't there a greater dedication to the dominion principle in healing the planet and restoring the whole world to sanity? I believe there are two reasons: (1) the lack of a centralized spiritual interest, and (2) competition currently outweighing cooperation. Let's take a closer look at each one.

The Centralized Interest Factor

For the majority of people, mind is like a computer out of control, with one low-vibration thought after another popping in and out — then being superimposed over other ideas and subsequently cancelled out by opposing thoughts in a jagged-ragged process of thinking. Interests are spread so thin that energy is scattered and thought-forms are only partially assembled before they begin to break up. And when there is a continuous trend of thought, the vibration is usually too low to be regarded as a *healing* influence.

Earlier I said that we are either healing or harming...there is no inbetween. Those with no centralized spiritual interest are actually in the latter category because they are non-contributors in the earth-healing process. Their attention jumps like a bouncing ball with the upswing emphasis on seeking happiness primarily through the acquisition of more material goods and status. Rarely are their energies used in service to others, and to broach the subject of world peace and planetary harmony brings little response. In short, there is no higher vision, no sense of global caring, no desire to enter into a *spiritual* way of life.

There is no condemnation of judgement involved here. I am simply describing how I see a great many third-dimensional men and women. Yet I can look at this group as a potential tidal wave of *good* for our world as they begin to awaken to the Truth within. You see, at the present time this low-vibratory species is desperately seeking fulfillment, but the object of the chase is only a phantom. And when they catch and embrace the phantom, they will find that it is only an illusion. This could certainly result in severe crises in their lives, but the potential emotional upheaval can be eased if a Seed of Truth is planted in their consciousness—to be retrieved from their memory banks at the proper time. And the planting of these Seeds is your responsibility...yours and every other Lightbearer.

How do you do this? First, by letting your fruits identify you as a Pathfinder and a Student of Truth—and then to share your Light with all who express even the slightest interest in your wholeness. Secondly, to not compromise your spiritual integrity by playing the low-vibration role when in the company of those with no spiritual interest. You must *live* your Truth every moment, regardless of where you find yourself, even if you have to do it silently! And thirdly, to take every opportunity to seed the mass consciousness by building and releasing thought-forms based on Truth and the divinity of every individual. This you do through meditation and spiritual treatment—and this activity will also offset the negative energy in the minds of those who are attacking progressive spiritual ideas and New Age concepts.

We are all one on the inner plane, and through your efforts you can play a major role in helping others to centralize their spiritual interest, energize their constructive thinking, and move up in consciousness to be a healing influence for our planet.

Competition Versus Cooperation

As far as I am concerned, there is no competition involved in the healing and harmonizing of Planet Earth. And no conflict of philosophies should keep us from supporting one another in this endeavor. Our objective, as you know, is to have 500-million people simply **consenting** to the healing of the planet— with no less than 50-million coming together in spirit at noon Greenwich time on December 31, 1986, and continuing to work together in a global Mind-Link until the last vestige of negative energy has been transmuted.

It is not absolutely necessary that participating individuals consider themselves to be members of the Planetary Commission if that identification is not relevant to their consciousness. And if another form of prayer or meditation is favored over the World Healing Meditation we hope that preference will not inhibit them from sharing their Light, Love and Energy on Healing Day. Whether the partiality is for the Commission Meditation, The Great Invocation, the Lord's Prayer, a particular Psalm, or a peace and healing meditation from the Holy Writings of Baha'i, Buddhism, Hinduism, or Islam, we know it will be the Divine Idea behind the words that will release the spiritual energy into the race consciousness.

What Jan and I have tried to convey since we announced the Commission on January 1, 1984, is that it does not belong to us or to The Quartus Foundation. It belongs to the world. There is no organizational structure or earthly hierarchy involved. The Commission is simply an umbrella under which millions are encouraged to gather and speak the Word for global healing. We seek no personal recognition relating to the Commission, nor do we feel that we are in competition with any other group or organization. We each have our pieces of the puzzle, so let's bring them together in a spirit of planetary cooperation and link our minds and hearts to heal the sense of separation and restore sanity to this planet.

With that thought in mind, I issue an invitation to all groups, organizations and individuals now sharing space on Earth and beyond to participate in what can be the greatest New Year's Eve Celebration in history.

Together we can transform Planet Earth.

Together we shall have . . . **DOMINION!**

APPENDIX

- Your Appointment to the Planetary Commission.

- The Time Where You Are at Noon Greenwich Time.

- The International Healing Meditation.

Please remove this page, date and sign it, note the country where you live, and mail to: The Quartus Foundation, P.O. Box 26683, Austin, Texas 78755.

I ACCEPT MY APPOINTMENT
TO THE PLANETARY COMMISSION

I choose to be a part of the Planetary Commission, and I do hereby consent to the healing and harmonizing of this planet and all forms of life hereon.

I shall begin this day to radiate the Infinite Spirit I AM in Truth to this world. I open my heart and I let Divine Love pour out to one and all, transmuting every negative situation and experience within the range of my consciousness.

I forgive everyone, including myself. I forgive the past and I close the door. From this moment on, I shall dedicate my life to turning within and seeking, finding, and knowing the only Presence, the only Power, the only Cause, and the only Activity of my eternal life. And I place my faith in the Presence of God within as my Spirit, my Substance, my Supply, and my Support.

I know that as I lift up my consciousness, I will be doing my part to cancel out the error of the race mind, heal the sense of separation, and restore the world to sanity.

With love in my heart, the thrill of victory in my mind, and joyous words on my lips, I agree to be a part of the world-wide group that will meet in spirit at noon Greenwich time on December 31, 1986, to release Light, Love and Spiritual Energy in the Healing Meditation for Planet Earth.

I now accept my appointment to the Planetary Commission!

_____   _____   _____

Date   Signature   Country

This is your copy of your Appointment to the Planetary Commission. Leave it in the book for frequent review and rededication.

I ACCEPT MY APPOINTMENT
TO THE PLANETARY COMMISSION

I choose to be a part of the Planetary Commission, and I do hereby consent to the healing and harmonizing of this planet and all forms of life hereon.

I shall begin this day to radiate the Infinite Spirit I AM in Truth to this world. I open my heart and I let Divine Love pour out to one and all, transmuting every negative situation and experience within the range of my consciousness.

I forgive everyone, including myself. I forgive the past and I close the door. From this moment on, I shall dedicate my life to turning within and seeking, finding, and knowing the only Presence, the only Power, the only Cause, and the only Activity of my eternal life. And I place my faith in the Presence of God within as my Spirit, my Substance, my Supply, and my Support.

I know that as I lift up my consciousness, I will be doing my part to cancel out the error of the race mind, heal the sense of separation, and restore the world to sanity.

With love in my heart, the thrill of victory in my mind, and joyous words on my lips, I agree to be a part of the worldwide group that will meet in spirit at noon Greenwich time on December 31, 1986, to release Light, Love and Spiritual Energy in the Healing Meditation for Planet Earth.

I now accept my appointment to the Planetary Commission!

| Date | Signature | Country |

TIME ZONES

The time where you are at noon Greenwich time.

United States Time Zones	Noon Greenwich Time
Pacific Standard Time	4:00 A.M.
Mountain Standard Time	5:00 A.M.
Central Standard Time	6:00 A.M.
Eastern Standard Time	7:00 A.M.

Noon Greenwich Time in Various Cities of the World

Berlin	1:00 P.M.	Montreal	7:00 A.M.
Buenos Aires	9:00 A.M.	Moscow	3:00 P.M.
Cairo	2:00 P.M.	Naples	1:00 P.M.
Copenhagen	1:00 P.M.	Nome	1:00 A.M.
Edmonton	5:00 A.M.	Ottawa	7:00 A.M.
Fairbanks	2:00 A.M.	Paris	1:00 P.M.
Glasgow	Noon	Rome	1:00 P.M.
Honolulu	2:00 A.M.	Sydney	10:00 P.M.
London	Noon	Tokyo	9:00 P.M.
Madrid	1:00 P.M.	Vancouver	4:00 A.M.
Mexico City	6:00 A.M.	Vienna	1:00 P.M.

WORLD HEALING MEDITATION

In the beginning
In the beginning *God*.
In the beginning God created the heaven and the earth.
And God said Let there be light: and there was light.

Now is the time of the *new* beginning.
I am a co-creator with God, and it is a new Heaven
    that comes,
as the Good Will of God is expressed on Earth through me.
It is the Kingdom of Light, Love, Peace and Understanding.
And I am doing my part to reveal its Reality.

I begin with me.
I am a living Soul and the Spirit of God dwells in me, as me.
I and the Father are one, and all that the Father has is mine.
In Truth, I am the Christ of God.

What is true of me is true of everyone,
for God is all and all is God.
I see only the Spirit of God in every Soul.
And to every man, woman and child on Earth I say:
I love you, for you are me. You are my Holy Self.

I now open my heart,
and let the pure essence of Unconditional Love pour out.
I see it as a Golden Light radiating from the center of
    my being,
and I feel its Divine Vibration in and through me, above
    and below me.

I am one with the Light.
I am filled with the Light.
I am illumined by the Light.
I am the Light of the world.

With purpose of mind, I send forth the Light.
I let the radiance go before me to join the other Lights.
I know this is happening all over the world at this moment.
I see the merging Lights.
There is now one Light. We are the Light of the world.

The one Light of Love, Peace and Understanding is moving.
It flows across the face of the Earth,
touching and illuminating every soul in the shadow of
    the illusion.
And where there was darkness, there is now the Light
    of Reality.

And the Radiance grows, permeating, saturating every
    form of life.
There is only the vibration of one Perfect Life now.
All the kingdoms of the Earth respond,
and the Planet is alive with Light and Love.

There is total Oneness,
and in this Oneness we speak the Word.
Let the sense of separation be dissolved.
Let mankind be returned to Godkind.

Let peace come forth in every mind.
Let Love flow forth from every heart.
Let forgiveness reign in every soul.
Let understanding be the common bond.

And now from the Light of the world,
the One Presence and Power of the Universe responds.
The Activity of God is healing and harmonizing
    Planet Earth.
Omnipotence is made manifest.

I am seeing the salvation of the planet before my very eyes,
as all false beliefs and error patterns are dissolved.
The sense of separation is no more; the healing has
    taken place,
and the world is restored to sanity.

This is the beginning of Peace on Earth and Good Will
    toward all,
as Love flows forth from every heart,
forgiveness reigns in every soul,
and all hearts and minds are one in perfect understanding.

It is done. And it is so.

NOTES

Chapter 1 – PROPHECY, PRINCIPLE AND PRAGMATISM

1. *The Woodrew Update*, published by the Space Technology and Research (S.T.A.R.) Foundation, 448 Rabbit Skin Road, Waynesville, N.C. 28786.

2. George W. Meek (compiled by), *Collapse & Comeback*, 1983, Metascience Foundation, Inc., P.O. Box 747, Franklin, N.C. 28734.

3. Greta Woodrew, *On A Slide of Light*, Macmillan Publishing Co., Inc. 1981. Available from S.T.A.R. Foundation, Inc. 448 Rabbit Skin Road, Waynesville, N.C. 28786.

4. John D. Hamaker (Selected Papers) & Donald A. Weaver (Annotations, Supporting Evidence), *The Survival of Civilization*, 1982, Hamaker-Weaver Publishers, Rt. 1, Box 158, Seymour, MO 65746 – or – P.O. Box 1961, Burlingame, CA 94010.

Chapter 5 – FROM FEARFUL TO FEARLESS

1. Djwhal Khul, the Tibetan, through Alice A. Bailey, *A Treatise on White Magic*, Lucis Publishing Company, Reference Edition 1967.

2. *A Course in Miracles*, Foundation for Inner Peace, 1975.

3. GREAT BOOKS OF THE WESTERN WORLD, Vol. 53, *William James*, published by Encyclopedia Britannica Inc., 1952.

Chapter 7 – WHAT ARE YOU SAYING AND SEEING?

1. Ernest Holmes, *The Science of Mind*, Dodd, Mean and Company, 1938.

2. Charles Fillmore, *Dynamics for Living*, Unity School of Christianity, 1967.

Chapter 9 – TWELVE DOORS TO MASTERY

1. Charles Fillmore, *The Twelve Powers of Man*, Unity School of Christianity, 1930.

2. Catherine Ponder, *The Healing Secret of the Ages*, Parker Publishing Company, Inc., 1967.

3. Rodney Collin, *The Theory of Celestial Influence*, Shambhala, 1984.

4. Samuel H. Sandweiss, M.D., *SAI BABA The Holy Man and the Psychiatrist*, Birthday Publishing Company, 1975.

5. Djwhal Khul, the Tibetan, through Alice A. Bailey, Vol. II – *Esoteric Psychology II*, Lucis Publishing Company, Reference Edition 1960.

6. *Metaphysical Bible Dictionary*, Unity School of Christianity, 1931.

Chapter 10 — QUESTIONS AND ANSWERS

1. H. Emilie Cady, *Lessons in Truth*, Unity School of Christianity, 1966.

2. Ferm M. Hook, *CHRIST TODAY LETTERS*, Christ Today Healing and Teaching Ministry, 34477 Hickory Lane, Lake Elsinore, CA 92330.

3. Ernest Holmes, *This Thing Called You*, Dodd, Mean & Company, 1948.

ABOUT THE AUTHOR

John Randolph Price is the president of The Quartus Foundation for Spiritual Research, Inc., a non-profit organization headquartered in the Texas hill country near Austin. His wife, Jan, co-founder of Quartus, is the executive director of the Foundation and also manages the group's publishing operations.

John and Jan have appeared on radio and television in major cities; have presented seminars in Unity, Religious Science, Divine Science, and independent New Thought churches, and have participated as keynote speakers and guest lecturers in symposiums sponsored by the International New Thought Alliance, the Association for Research and Enlightenment, and other metaphysical groups. Their backgrounds in spiritual research and the application of metaphysical principles span nearly 20 years.

Prior to the founding of Quartus, John was a consultant to business and industry, president of a Houston-based communications firm, and executive vice president of a Chicago and New York advertising agency. He has written and produced documentaries for the U.S. Government and television programs for public broadcasting. He also devoted considerable time to writing and lecturing on the human potential movement. He is a graduate of the University of Houston.

In addition to *Practical Spirituality*, John has authored *The Superbeings, The Planetary Commission,* and *The Manifestation Process: 10 Steps to the Fulfillment of Your Desires.*

The Quartus Foundation

The Quartus Foundation for Spiritual Research is an organization dedicated to research and communications on the divinity of man. We seek to study the records of the past, investigate events and experiences of the present, and probe the possibilities and potential of the future through the illumined consciousness of awakened Souls.

Our objective is to continually document the truth that man is a spiritual being possessing all of the powers of the spiritual realm . . . that man is indeed God individualized, and that as man realizes his true identity, he becomes a Master Mind with dominion over the material world.

The documentation comes through indepth research into case histories of the past and present, which reveal the healing, prospering, harmonizing Power of God working in and through man. We believe that man is capable of rising above every problem and challenge that could possibly beset him, and that he is doing this daily in ways that are considered both "mysterious and miraculous." But in truth, the evil, the illness, the failure, the limitation, the danger, the injustice disappear through a change in individual consciousness. What brought about the change? We seek to examine closely the problem and the solution, the activity of Mind and the Law of Mind, the cause and effect — and to build a fund of knowledge based on the interrelationship of Spirit, Soul, Body, and the world of form and experience.

We believe that what one person is doing to alter conditions and reveal order and harmony, all can do — and by researching and communicating specific examples of man's inherent powers, we can do our part in assisting in the general upliftment of consciousness. Through greater understanding, we can all develop a more dynamic faith in our inner Self, a conviction that our potential is only limited by the scope of our vision, and a Knowledge that mankind is Godkind and does not have to accept anything less than heaven on earth.

For complete details on the activities of The Quartus Foundation, write for your free copy of The Quartus Report, P.O. Box 26683, Austin, Texas 78755.

BOOKS AND TAPES AVAILABLE FROM THE QUARTUS FOUNDATION

- *Practical Spirituality*
  by John Randolph Price $6.95

- *The Planetary Commission*
  by John Randolph Price $7.95
  Truth Seekers and Pathfinders from all of the threads of
  the Golden Cord (the metaphysical factor in all reli-
  gions) are uniting again—this time in a New Commission to reveal the Light of the World. Included is the
  Commission Workbook for Self-Mastery featuring lessons and spiritual exercises to help you rediscover
  your self.

- *The Superbeings*
  by John Randolph Price $5.95
  Men and women in all walks of life are rapidly evolving
  toward undreamed of powers . . . some have reached
  the point of mastery where they are no longer bound
  by the ills, limitations and problems of this world.
  Their secrets are revealed in this exciting book so that
  you, too, may develop and use the miracle power of
  the Supermind.

- *The Manifestation Process: 10 Steps to the
  Fulfillment of Your Desires*
  by John Randolph Price $3.95
  This booklet is an expanded version of the process
  taught in the early Superbeing Seminars, and is based
  on a concept originally developed after closely evaluat-
  ing the consciousness characteristics of a number of
  highly evolved individuals. Each principle is discussed,
  and the reader is led through a meditative treatment to
  duplicate the automatic activity of Superbeing Consciousness in a step-by-step process.

- *Journey of Love* by Alan Mesher $6.95
  A combination of personal experiences, spiritual teachings and meditative practices that will help the reader
  develop and bring forth the power, fulfillment and
  mastery from within.

Cassette Tapes

By John Price
- *The 40-day Prosperity Plan—*
  including the technique of how to
  listen to your money talk $6.95
- *The Future Is Now*—from Chapter One of *The Plane-*
  tary Commission—Discusses the critical opportunity
  before us to heal and harmonize the planet, and
  includes the Healing Meditation $6.95
- *The Incredible Power of Love* $6.95
- *Developing Mastery Through Faith,*
  Strength and Wisdom $6.95
- *The Manifestation Process—*
  companion to the booklet
  with the Manifestation Meditation $9.95

By Jan Price
- *Releasing and Infilling Meditations* $5.95
- *Have a Love Affair with Your Self* $6.95
- *The Miracle Working Power of At-One-Ment* $6.95

Please add $1.00 for postage and handling. Texas resi-
dents add 5¹/8% Sales Tax.
Order from: The Quartus Foundation, P.O. Box 26683,
Austin, Texas 78755